The Aquinas Catechism

Other books
by St. Thomas Aquinas
from Sophia Institute Press:

The Aquinas Prayer Book
Aquinas's Shorter Summa
The Ways of God

St. Thomas Aquinas

The Aquinas Catechism

A Simple Explanation of the Catholic Faith
by the Church's Greatest Theologian

SOPHIA INSTITUTE PRESS®
Manchester, New Hampshire

The material in *The Aquinas Catechism* was previously published as two books: *The Three Greatest Prayers* (Manchester, New Hampshire: Sophia Institute Press, 1990) and *God's Greatest Gifts* (Manchester, New Hampshire: Sophia Institute Press, 1992).

Jacket design by Lorraine Bilodeau

On the cover: *Jesus' Miracles* from *Stories of St. John the Baptist* fresco, by Giusto di Giovanni Menabuoi, O.P. (1363-1393), Italian Baptistry of the Cathedral, Padua / SuperStock.

Sophia Institute Press®
Box 5284, Manchester, NH 03108
1-800-888-9344
www.sophiainstitute.com

Library of Congress Cataloging-in-Publication Data

Thomas, Aquinas, Saint, 1225?-1274.
  The Aquinas catechism : a simple explanation of the Catholic faith by the Church's greatest theologian / St. Thomas Aquinas.
      p. cm.
  Previously published as two separate works under the titles: The three greatest prayers; God's greatest gifts, in 1990 and 1992.
    ISBN 1-928832-10-5 (pbk. : alk. paper)
    1. Lord's Prayer. 2. Ave Maria. 3. Apostles' Creed. I. Thomas, Aquinas, Saint, 1225?-1274. Three greatest prayers. II. Thomas, Aquinas, Saint, 1225?-1274. De decem praeceptis. English. III. Title.
  BX890.T62 E6 2000
  230'.2 — dc21   00-035754

CONTENTS

2. HOW CHRISTIANS SHOULD PRAY

4. HOW THE CHURCH NOURISHES CHRISTIANS

Editor's note: The biblical quotations in the following pages are based on the Douay-Rheims edition of the Old and New Testaments. Where applicable, quotations have been cross-referenced with the differing names and enumeration in the Revised Standard Version, using the following symbol: (RSV =). Quotations from the Douay-Rheims translation that are obscure in their meaning have been replaced with the equivalent quotation from the Revised Standard Version.

FOREWORD
Ralph McInerny, Ph.D.
The Michael P. Grace Professor of Medieval Studies
University of Notre Dame

St. Thomas Aquinas preached a series of sermons during Lent in 1273, the last year of his life. Delivered in the church of San Domenico in Naples in Thomas's native Neapolitan dialect (rather than in Latin), the sermons were directed to the simple faithful and had an immediate and profound impact on those who heard them.

We are told by a contemporary Neapolitan (John Coppa) that "almost the whole population of Naples went to hear his sermons every day." And William of Tocco writes that "he was heard by the people with such reverence that it was as if his preaching came forth from God."

Summaries of the sermons were made by Reginald of Piperno and have come down to us in Latin, often touched up to make them look more academic than the popular sermons they origi-nally were. Thus we do not have verbatim transcripts of them or even Thomas's own written version of what he said. But what we have is sufficient to see why the faithful in large numbers re-sponded as they did.

Even today and in English translation, these sermons speak as directly to believers as they did when they were first delivered.

The sermons are remarkable for their clarity, their depth, their holiness, and their wealth of scriptural quotations. As a result, although they have had a more checkered history than that of Thomas's other works, they have always held a special place in the hearts of the faithful — experts and laymen — for they address all men quite simply and directly as Christian believers.

Part of St. Thomas's universal popularity comes from his mastery of each of the threefold tasks of the medieval theologian: lecturing, disputing, and preaching.

Lecturing meant reading and commenting on Scripture and on major theological treatises to give an orderly presentation of Christian doctrine and of the comments of the Fathers of the Church on it.

Disputing meant sustaining theses and handling objections to them in the great public debates that characterized the medieval university. (To his formal disputations we owe Thomas's *Disputed Questions* and his *Quodlibetal Questions*. His *Summa Theologica* and *Summa Contra Gentiles*, like his commentaries on the works of Aristotle, were not products of the classroom but of his private enterprise as a Master of Theology.)

Preaching was the third and (to moderns, at least) the least *well-known* of the tasks of the medieval theologian. Yet, as can be seen from the sermons published here, the sermons of the medieval theologian reflect all of the wisdom gained from lecturing and disputing in the university.

Thus, for example, because they give us such a concise and edifying overview of the Faith, Thomas's sermons on the Apostles' Creed could be called "a *Summa* for the simple." These sermons lead us to turn over in our minds and hearts the great articles of the Faith in much the same way as the Mysteries of the Rosary provide us with a vivid summary of the history of salvation.

Or consider Thomas's opening remarks on the Lord's Prayer. There is surely no surprise in the fact that Thomas considers the most perfect prayer to be the one that Jesus taught His followers when they asked Him how to pray. Anyone might make the same judgment.

Thomas, however, goes on to show us *why* it is so perfect by listing the five conditions necessary to prayer and showing how the Lord's Prayer fulfills them all in a preeminent manner. He then indicates that prayer brings about three goods and shows how the Lord's Prayer is particularly efficacious in bringing about all three.

You can hear the university lecturer in such remarks, but it is also the voice of the catechist who wants to make as plain as he can the great truths of salvation.

Although great scholarship is presupposed for such analysis, the most immediately evident characteristic of these sermons is their wealth of quotations, primarily from Scripture (both Old and New Testaments) but also from the Fathers of the Church, our predecessors in the journey toward Heaven.

This also should not be surprising, for the medieval theologian had to know the Bible by heart, not only because copies of it were so prohibitively expensive but also as a professional necessity: the Scriptures are the chief source of the theologian's inspiration and he must turn to them time and again for light.

Consequently, the reader of this book is given a *florilegium* of biblical passages as well as numerous citations from Fathers of the Church, such as Augustine and Cyprian, all of which cast light on the prayers about which Thomas is preaching.

Such prodigious scholarship alone would not suffice to make these commentaries worthy of the attention of both scholars and laymen. Their universal appeal is explained by yet another fact: Thomas Aquinas was not only the most learned man of his time; he was also a saint.

In common with the other Doctors of the Church, Thomas had achieved in his life a union of learning and sanctity. When he stood in the pulpit of San Domenico on those Lenten days in 1273 and spoke from his heart to his fellow Christians, he was speaking of the one great task we all share: to become perfect as our heavenly Father is perfect.

Contrast this with the thoroughly modern theologian who insists that his task must be sharply distinguished from that of the pastor. The theologian, we are told today, is a university person, not a catechist. For Thomas, however, the theologian was pursuing the common Christian vocation of holiness: it would be an abomination to be learned in the things of God and not, in one's own life, to pursue in grace friendship with God. (For this reason, the Church puts before us many models of sanctity who were not learned persons, but it has never accorded special status to Christians who were learned but not holy.)

Although he was the greatest scholar of his time, Thomas treasured holiness far more than scholarship. This is evident from an incident that occurred during the same Lent in which these sermons were preached. One day, Thomas was observed praying in the chapel of St. Nicholas at the Naples monastery. A voice from the crucifix spoke: "Thomas, you have written well of me. What would you have as a reward for your work?" And Thomas answered: "Lord, only Thyself."

It is well to remind ourselves of such stories of Thomas's sanctity which refer to the very period in which these sermons were preached. Yes, Thomas had the acquired wisdom of the scholar; but far more important, he had that wisdom which is a gift of the Holy Spirit. Both wisdoms are evident in these sermons, but it is the second that gives them that ring of holiness which establishes their universal appeal and their enduring significance for us.

Today, publication of such a book of sermons may not set a trend; but no matter. And even among those who do pick up this book, many may read it solely to learn about the sermon as a literary genre or to add to their scholarly knowledge of St. Thomas and the Middle Ages.

This would be unfortunate, for although the sermon is certainly a literary genre, it is much more than that. And although these particular sermons reveal much about St. Thomas and the Middle Ages, they do far more than that.

One of the Fathers of the Church said that "God did not become man in order that man might become a theologian." Similarly, St. Thomas did not preach these sermons to exemplify a literary genre or to provide a new footnote on the Middle Ages. He preached these sermons to lead his hearers to holiness.

For those still striving for holiness, the publication of these sermons — by this author on prayers such as these — is a grace indeed.

EDITOR'S PREFACE

In the spirit of St. Thomas, who intended these Lenten sermons for the unlettered as well as the lettered, I have prepared this edition specifically to introduce the wisdom of this great saint and theologian to the average modern reader.

Most people — laymen and scholars alike — find that their first obstacle in reading St. Thomas is the richness of his texts. You will discover that even in these sermons for the average man, St. Thomas has included so many points that it is easy to get lost. To help you overcome this obstacle and profit from this incredibly rich text, I have made a number of significant changes to the 1937 and 1939 English editions on which this present edition is based.

First, I have adopted a somewhat unique format. Where necessary, I have added headings and subheadings (in bold-face type) and have sometimes also rendered in bold-face type the beginnings of paragraphs. Although this latter may seem typographically odd, it serves an important function: bold-faced passages constitute an outline within the text itself and also correspond directly to entries found in the more detailed outlines in the Appendix. If you follow the outlines as you read the text, you will never lose your place, and will see relations between passages that might otherwise not be apparent.

In addition to adopting a unique format, I have taken other steps to increase this text's readability: some of the longer sentences have been shortened; implied referents have often been made specific; extremely awkward formulations have been paraphrased; and the archaic language of the 1937 and 1939 English editions has been changed into standard modern English.

Where possible, I have given more precise references than were found in the earlier editions. Where that edition indicated that passages are quotations but failed to provide a source, I have retained quotation marks, but have similarly indicated no source.

It must be understood, above all, that *this is not a scholarly edition, nor does it pretend to be*. Scholars should be reading these sermons in Latin! This edition is for the average person who seeks to know more about his Faith and to grow holy.

Read it slowly, attentively, and prayerfully. You will soon discover why St. Thomas Aquinas was proclaimed a Doctor of the Universal Church in 1567 and why he has been revered as a master theologian for seven centuries.

More important, you yourself will grow wise in your Faith, and, if you persist in living by that wisdom, you will come to be like St. Thomas not only in wisdom, but in holiness.

The Aquinas Catechism

Part 1

What Christians Believe

The Apostles' Creed

THE APOSTLES' CREED

I believe in God, the Father almighty,
Creator of Heaven and earth;
and in Jesus Christ, His only Son, our Lord
who was conceived by the Holy Spirit
and born of the Virgin Mary.
He suffered under Pontius Pilate,
was crucified, died, and was buried.
He descended into Hell.
On the third day He rose again from the dead.
He ascended into Heaven,
and is seated at the right hand of God,
the Father almighty.
From thence He shall come
to judge the living and the dead.
I believe in the Holy Spirit,
the holy Catholic Church,
the communion of saints,
the forgiveness of sins,
the resurrection of the body,
and life everlasting. Amen.

I BELIEVE IN GOD, THE FATHER ALMIGHTY, CREATOR OF HEAVEN AND EARTH

A. Faith

The first thing a Christian needs is faith, without which no man is a faithful Christian. Faith confers four benefits:

1. Faith unites the soul to God, because by faith the Christian soul is in a sense wedded to God: "I will espouse thee to myself in faith."[1] For this reason, when we are baptized, we begin by confessing our Faith when we are asked, "Do you believe in God?" For Baptism is the first of the sacraments of faith. Hence our Lord said, "He that believeth and is baptized, shall be saved"[2] since without faith, Baptism is of no avail.

Consequently, we must realize that without faith no man is acceptable to God: "Without faith it is impossible to please God."[3] For this reason (commenting on Rom. 14:23: "All that is not of faith is sin"), St. Augustine says, "Without the recognition of the eternal and unchangeable truth, all virtue is but a sham even in the best of men."

---

[1] Osee 2:20 (RSV = Hos. 2:20).
[2] Mark 16:16.
[3] Heb. 11:6.

2. Faith introduces eternal life into us, for eternal life is nothing else than to know God. Thus our Lord said, "This is eternal life, to know Thee, the only true God."[4] This knowledge of God begins in us by faith, and is perfected in the life to come, when we shall know Him as He is: "Faith is the substance of things to be hoped for."[5] So no man can obtain the happiness of Heaven — which is the true knowledge of God — unless he knows Him first by faith: "Blessed are they that have not seen, and have believed."[6]

3. Faith is our guide in the present life, since in order to lead a good life a man needs to know what is necessary to live rightly. (If he had to rely on his own efforts to discover all that is necessary for that purpose, either he would never discover it or he would only do so after a long time.) But faith teaches us all that is necessary for leading a good life, since we learn by faith that there is one God who is the rewarder of the good and the punisher of the wicked; that there is another life besides this; and other such truths by which we are sufficiently drawn to do good and avoid evil: "The just shall live in his faith."[7] This is also shown from the fact that before the coming of Christ none of the philosophers was able, however great his effort, to know as much about God or about the means necessary for obtaining eternal life, as any old woman knows by faith since Christ came down upon earth. And therefore it is said in Isaiah, "The earth is filled with knowledge of God."[8]

---

[4] John 17:3.
[5] Heb. 11:1.
[6] John 20:29.
[7] Hab. 2:4.
[8] Isa. 11:9.

4. Faith helps us overcome temptations: "[The saints] by faith have conquered kingdoms."[9] The reason is that all temptation is from either the Devil, the world, or the flesh.

a. The Devil tempts us to disobey God and to refuse to be subject to Him. This temptation is removed by faith, since faith teaches us that He is the Lord of all, which is why we must obey Him: "Your adversary the Devil . . . goeth about seeking whom he may devour: whom resist ye strong in faith."[10]

b. The world tempts us either by the attractions of prosperity or by fear of adversity. We overcome these temptations by faith because it teaches that there is a better life than this, so that we despise the good things of this world and do not fear its afflictions: "This is the victory which overcometh the world, our faith."[11] We also overcome these temptations by faith because it teaches us there are evils still greater than temptation, namely, those of Hell.

c. The flesh tempts us by drawing us to the passing pleasures of this life. But faith teaches us that if we seek them unduly we shall forfeit eternal happiness: "In all things putting on the shield of faith."[12] Hence we gather how profitable it is to have faith.

5. Faith is not foolish. But someone might object that it is foolish to believe what is not seen, and that one should not believe

9   Heb. 11:33.
10   1 Pet. 5:8, 9.
11   1 John 5:4.
12   Cf. Eph. 6:16.

what one does not see. I reply that this difficulty disappears if we consider the following points:

a. **Because our intelligence is imperfect.** If we were able by ourselves to know perfectly all things, visible and invisible, it would be foolish for us to believe what we do not see. But our knowledge is so imperfect that no philosopher has ever been able to discover perfectly the nature of a single fly. We are told that a certain philosopher spent thirty years in solitude in the endeavor to know the nature of the bee. If our intelligence is so weak, is it not foolish to be willing to believe about God only what we are able to find out by ourselves alone? In fact, this is condemned by the words of Job: "Behold, God is great, exceeding our knowledge."[13]

b. **Because our knowledge is limited.** Another reason why faith is not foolish concerns expertise. If an expert were to make a statement in his own particular branch of knowledge, an uneducated person would be a fool if he contradicted the expert for no other reason than that he could not understand what the expert had said. Now, without a doubt, the intelligence of an angel surpasses that of the greatest philosopher far more than the intelligence of the philosopher surpasses that of an ignoramus. Therefore, a philosopher is a fool to disbelieve what an angel says, and a much greater fool if he disbelieves what God says. He is condemned in the words of Ecclus. 3:25: "Many things are shown to Thee above the understanding of men."

c. **Because life in this world would be altogether impossible if one were only to believe what one sees.** How can one

[13] Job 36:26.

live without believing others? How is a man to believe that so-and-so is his father? Man has to believe others in matters that he cannot know perfectly by himself.

Now no one is to be believed as much as God is. Thus, those who will not believe the statements of faith are not wise, but foolish and proud. As the Apostle[14] says, "He is proud, knowing nothing;[15] and, "I know whom I have believed; and I am certain."[16] And it is written, "Ye who fear the Lord, believe Him."[17]

d. Because God's miracles prove the truth of the things which faith teaches. Thus if a king sends a letter to which he has attached his seal, no one will dare say this letter was not written by the king's orders. Now, it is plain that whatever the saints have believed and handed down to us concerning the Christian Faith is confirmed by God's seal, which is to be seen in those works which no mere creature is able to do, namely, the miracles by which Christ confirmed the doctrine of the Apostles and of other saints.

And if anyone says that nobody has seen those miracles done, I reply that it is a well-known fact, related in pagan histories, that the whole world worshiped idols and persecuted the Christian Faith; yet now, behold all (the wise, the noble, the rich, the powerful, and the great) have been converted by the words of a few simple poor men who preached Christ.

Now was this a miracle or was it not?

---

[14] St. Thomas uses *the Apostle* to refer to St. Paul.

[15] 1 Tim. 6:4.

[16] 2 Tim. 1:12.

[17] Ecclus. 2:8 (RSV = Sir. 2:8).

If it was, then you have what you asked for. If you say it was not a miracle, then I say that you could not have a greater miracle than the conversion of the whole world without miracles, and we need seek no further. Accordingly no one should doubt about the Faith, and we should believe what is of faith even more than the things that we see, since man's sight may be deceived, whereas God's knowledge is never at fault.

B. The nature and work of God

The first of all the articles of Faith is that the faithful must believe in one God.[18]

1. God governs all things. It will be well to consider what is meant by this word God, for it signifies the governor and provider of all things. To believe there is a God is to believe in one whose government and Providence extend to all things, whereas one who believes that all things happen by chance does not believe there is a God.

a. God governs nature. No one, however, is so foolish as not to believe that the things of the physical world are subject to someone's government, providence, and disposition, seeing that they are regulated according to a certain order and time. For we see the sun, the moon, the stars, and other parts of the physical world all holding a certain course, which would not happen if they were the sport of chance.

Therefore a man would be a fool not to believe in God: "The fool hath said in his heart, 'There is no God.' "[19]

[18] The word one was added in the Nicene Creed.
[19] Ps. 13:1 (RSV = Ps. 14:1).

b. God governs human actions. Some there are, however, who, although they believe that nature is governed and ordained by God, deny that human actions come under His Providence. They believe, in fact, that human actions are not disposed by God. Their reason is that they see that in this world the good suffer and the wicked prosper, which would seem to argue against God's Providence in regard to mankind. Thus it is said in their person, "He walks about the poles of Heaven; nor does He consider our things."[20] But this is very foolish. They behave like one who knows nothing about medicine, and who, seeing the physician prescribing water for one invalid and wine for another (according to the requirements of the medical art), believes this to be done haphazardly, whereas it is the medical art which with good reason prescribes water for the one and wine for the other.

It is the same with God, who with good cause and by His Providence disposes such things as are necessary to man. Thus He afflicts some good men and allows certain wicked men to prosper. Anyone who believes this to be the result of chance is (and is reputed to be) a fool, since the sole cause of his conviction is that he does not know the art and reason of the divine disposition: "Would that He might show thee the secrets of wisdom, and that His law is manifold."[21]

We must, therefore, firmly believe that God governs and disposes not only the things of nature but also the acts of men: "And they have said: The Lord shall not see; neither shall the God of Jacob understand. Understand, ye senseless among the people; and ye fools, be wise at last. He that planted the ear, shall He not hear? Or He that formed the

---

[20] Cf. Job 22:14.
[21] Job 11:6.

11

eye, shall He not consider? . . . The Lord knoweth the thoughts of men."[22]

He sees all things, our thoughts, and the secrets of our will. For this reason men are placed under a special obligation of doing good, since all their thoughts and deeds are manifest to the all-seeing God. Hence the Apostle says, "All things are naked and open to His eyes."[23]

2. There is only one God. Moreover, we must believe that this God who disposes and rules all things is but one God. This is because human affairs are found to be rightly disposed when many things are subject to the disposition and government of one. A multitude of heads often produces dissension among the subjects. Therefore, since the divine government surpasses human government, it is evident that the world must be governed not by many gods, but by one only.

a. Reasons for belief in many gods (polytheism). Four motives led men to believe in many gods:

1. The weakness of our human intelligence was the first, the result being that through inability to transcend the corporeal world, men did not believe there was any nature besides that of sensible bodies. Consequently, they held that the world is disposed and ruled by those bodies which they observed to surpass all others in beauty and nobility (the sun, moon, and stars) to which accordingly they attributed and paid divine worship.

These men are like those who, when going to court to see the king, think anyone who is well-dressed or

[22] Ps. 93:7-9, 11 (RSV = Ps. 94:7-9, 11).
[23] Heb. 4:13.

who exercises an office to be the king. Of such men Wisdom says, "They have imagined . . . the sun and moon . . . or the circle of the stars to be the gods that rule the world."[24] And Isaiah says, "Lift up your eyes to Heaven and look down to the earth beneath; for the Heavens shall vanish like smoke, and the earth shall be worn away like a garment, and the inhabitants thereof shall perish in like manner. But my salvation shall be forever, and my justice shall not fail."[25]

2. Human flattery was the second motive for polytheism. Some men, desiring to flatter their masters and sovereigns, gave them the honor due to God by obeying them and subjecting themselves to them, making gods of them when they were dead, or even while yet in life: "Let every nation know that Nebuchadnezzar is god upon the earth, and beside him is no other."[26]

3. Carnal affection for children and kindred was a third motive for polytheism. Thus some, through an excessive love for their own relatives, raised statues to them after they had died, the result being that they paid divine honor to these statues. Of these it is said: "Men serving either their affection or their kings gave the incommunicable name to stones and wood."[27]

4. The wickedness of the Devil was a fourth cause of polytheism. He it was who from the beginning desired

[24] Wisd. 13:2.
[25] Isa. 51:6.
[26] Jth. 5:29.
[27] Wisd. 14:21.

to be equal to God. Thus he says, "I will place my throne in the north; I will ascend above the height of the clouds; I will be like the Most High."[28] This desire he has never put aside, which is why he strives his utmost to be worshiped by men and to have sacrifices offered to himself.

Not that he is pleased in the dog or cat that is offered to him, but he is pleased in being paid the reverence due to God. Hence he said to Christ, "All these things will I give Thee if falling down Thou wilt adore me."[29] With this purpose the demons entered idols and answered when questioned, that they might be reverenced as gods: "The idols of the Gentiles are silver and gold."[30] Thus the Apostle says, "The things which the heathens sacrifice, they sacrifice to devils and not to God."[31]

b. Who are the polytheists? Now all this is horrible, yet from time to time there have been some to whom these four causes apply. Not in word or thought, but in deed they show that they believe in many gods:

1. Those who believe that Heavenly bodies influence the human will, and who choose certain seasons for their actions, make gods and rulers of the heavenly bodies and cast horoscopes: "Be not afraid of the signs from heaven which the heathens fear, for the laws of the people are vain."[32]

---

[28] Isa. 14:13, 14.

[29] Matt. 4:9.

[30] Ps. 113:4 (RSV = Ps. 115:4).

[31] 1 Cor. 10:20.

[32] Jer. 10:2, 3.

2. Those who obey kings rather than God, in matters where they ought not to obey them, make kings their gods: "We ought to obey God rather than men."[33]

3. Those who love their children or kindred more than God imply by their deeds that there are many gods.

4. Those who love the pleasures of the table more than God, and of whom the Apostle says, "whose God is their belly."[34]

5. Those who engage in sorcery and incantations treat the demons as if they were gods, since they seek to obtain from the demons that which God alone can give, namely, knowledge of the occult and the truth about future events.

We must, therefore, believe that there is but one God.

3. God created Heaven and earth. As stated above, the first thing that we must believe is that there is but one God. The second is that this God is the Creator and Maker of Heaven and earth, of things visible and invisible. Without having recourse to subtle explanations, it is enough for our present purpose to illustrate by means of a homely example the fact that all things were created and made by God.

Suppose a man entering a house were to feel heat on the porch, and on going further, were to feel the heat increasing, the more he penetrated within. Doubtless, he would believe there was a fire in the house, even though he did not see the fire that must be causing all this heat.

[33] Acts 5:29.
[34] Phil. 3:19.

A similar thing will happen to anyone who considers this world in detail: he will observe that all things are arranged according to their degrees of beauty and excellence, and that the nearer they are to God, the more beautiful and the better they are. The heavenly bodies are more beautiful and more noble than the bodies of the lower world, and invisible things are more beautiful and noble than visible.

Which is why we must believe that all these things come from one God who gives each thing its being and excellence. Wisdom says, "All men are vain in whom there is not the knowledge of God; and who, by these good things that are seen, cannot understand Him that is. By attending to the works, they have not acknowledged Him who was the workman."[35] And further on: "By the greatness of the beauty, and of the creature, the Creator of them may be seen so as to be known thereby."[36] We must, therefore, take it as clearly demonstrated that all the things that are in the world come from God.

a. Errors concerning creation
In relation to this truth, three errors are to be avoided:

1. The error of the Manicheans, who say that all things visible were created by the Devil. Thus they assert that God created only invisible things. They fell into this error because, while holding that God is the sovereign good (which is true), they held that whatever comes from good must itself be good and also (through not knowing how to discern what is good and what is evil), they believed that whatever is in any way evil, is altogether evil. For instance, they said that fire (because it

[35] Wisd. 13:1.
[36] Wisd. 13:5.

burns) and water (because it suffocates) are essentially
evil, and so on. Therefore, seeing that none of these sensible things is simply good, but each is in some way evil
and defective, they asserted that visible things were not
made by the good God, but by an evil god.

Arguing against the Manicheans, St. Augustine em-
ploys the following example. If a man were to enter a
smith's forge and injure himself by colliding with the
smith's tools and then blame the smith for his wickedness in possessing such tools, he would be a fool, since
the smith has those tools for his work. Even so is it foolish
to say that a creature is evil because in some way it is
harmful, since what is harmful to one is useful to another.
This error is contrary to the Church's Faith, and therefore we speak of *all things visible and invisible*.[37] ("In the beginning God created Heaven and earth."[38] "All things
were made by Him."[39])

**2. The error of those who say the world has existed
from eternity,** in reference to which Peter says, "Since
the time that the fathers slept, all things continue as they
were from the beginning of the creation."[40] They were led
into this error by not knowing how to imagine the world
having a beginning. Referring to these, Rabbi Moses says
they are like a man placed on an island immediately after
his birth, who remains ignorant of the manner of preg-
nancy and childbirth. After he has grown up, when
someone tells him how man is conceived, carried in the

[37] In the Nicene Creed.
[38] Gen. 1:1.
[39] John 1:3.
[40] 2 Pet. 3:4.

womb, and born into the world, he refuses to believe his informant because he deems it impossible for a man to be in his mother's womb. In the same way and in view of the present state of the world, some people do not believe that the world had a beginning.

This also is contrary to the Church's Faith, and so to reject this we say: *Creator of Heaven and earth*,[41] since if they were made, it goes without saying that they did not always exist. Hence we read in the Psalm, "He spoke and they were made."[42]

3. The error of those who asserted that God made the world from pre-existing matter. They were led to their position through wishing to measure God's power by our own power. Seeing that man can make nothing without pre-existing matter, they believed that it is the same with God. Consequently, they said that in producing things, God had pre-existing matter at His disposal. But this is not true. For man is unable to make anything without pre-existing matter since he is a particular maker, and can only introduce this or that form into this or that matter which is presupposed from another source.

This is because a man's power is confined to the form only, and consequently his causality is confined to the production of this or that form. On the other hand, God is the universal Cause of all things, and creates not only the form, but also the matter. He made all things out of nothing.

Therefore, to reject this position we say, *Creator of Heaven and earth*. For *to create* and *to make* differ in that *to*

[41] In the Nicene Creed.
[42] Ps. 148:5.

create is to make something out of nothing. Consequently, if God made something out of nothing we must believe that He can remake all things if they happen to be destroyed. He can give sight to the blind, raise the dead to life, and work other similar miracles: "For Thy power is at hand when Thou wilt."[43]

b. Benefits of belief in God as Creator

Belief in God as Creator affords us five benefits:

1. It leads us to a knowledge of the divine majesty, because the maker is greater than the things he makes. Since God is the Maker of all things, it follows that He is greater than all things: "With whose beauty, if they being delighted took them to be gods, let them know how much the Lord of them is more beautiful than they. . . . Or if they admired their power and their effects, let them understand by them that He who made them is mightier than they."[44] Think or imagine whatever we will, it is less than God: "God is great, exceeding our knowledge."[45]

2. It leads us to give thanks to God. Since God is the Creator of all things, it is certain that all that we *are* and all that we *have* come from God. Thus the Apostle says, "What hast thou that thou hast not received?"[46] And the Psalm says, "The earth is the Lord's and the fullness thereof, the world and all they that dwell therein."[47]

[43] Wisd. 12:18.
[44] Wisd. 13:3, 4.
[45] Job 36:26.
[46] 1 Cor. 4:7.
[47] Ps. 23:1 (RSV = Ps. 24:1).

19

For this reason we owe Him thanksgiving: "What shall I render unto the Lord for all the things that He has rendered to me?"[48]

3. It encourages us to be patient in adversity. For although all creatures come from God and therefore are good as regards their nature, yet if in any way they harm us and bring us pain, we must believe the punishment is from God (but not that which is sinful, because no evil comes from God except insofar as it is directed to a good). Consequently, if all the pains a man suffers come from God, he must bear them patiently. For by pain sins are cleansed, the guilty are humbled, and the good are urged on to the love of God: "If we have received good things at the Lord's hands, why should we not receive evil?"[49]

4. It persuades us to use creatures well, because we ought to employ creatures for the purpose to which God made them. Now this purpose is twofold: for the glory of God (since "the Lord hath made all things for Himself,"[50] i.e., for His own glory) and for our profit ("Which the Lord thy God created for the service of all the nations"[51]). We must, therefore, make use of things for God's glory in a way that pleases God and also profits ourselves, so as to avoid sin in using them: "All things are Thine; and we have given Thee what we have received from Thy hand."[52] Hence whatever you have, be

[48] Ps. 115:12 (RSV = Ps. 116:12).
[49] Job. 2:10.
[50] Prov. 16:4.
[51] Deut. 4:19.
[52] 1 Paralip. 29:14 (RSV = 1 Chron. 29:14).

it knowledge or beauty, you must refer all and use all for the glory of God.

5. It leads us to acknowledge man's dignity, because God made all things for man's sake: "Thou hast subjected all things under his feet."[53] Moreover, after the angels, man of all creatures is most like God: "Let us make man to our own image and likeness."[54] He did not say this of the Heaven or of the stars, but of man — not, indeed, as regards man's body, but as regards his soul, which is endowed with a free will and is incorruptible, and in which he resembles God more than other creatures do.

We must, therefore, realize that after the angels, man excels all other creatures, and that in no way must we forfeit our dignity on account of sin or for the sake of an inordinate desire for corporeal things which are beneath us and made to serve us. We must conduct ourselves according to the purpose for which God made us, seeing that He made man to preside over all things on earth and to be subject to Himself. Accordingly, we must rule and hold dominion over the things of the earth, but we must be subject to God by obeying and serving Him, and so we shall attain to the enjoyment of God.

May He grant that this be so.

---

[53] Ps. 8:8 (RSV = Ps. 8:6).
[54] Gen. 1:26.

II

AND IN JESUS CHRIST,
HIS ONLY SON, OUR LORD

A. Christ is the Son of God

Not only must Christians believe in one God, and that He is the Creator of Heaven and earth and of all things, but they must also believe that God is the Father, of whom Christ is the true Son.

1. The scriptural evidence. As St. Peter says in his second canonical epistle, this is no fable, but an ascertained fact proved by the voice on the mountain: "For we have not by following artificial fables made known to you the power and the presence of our Lord Jesus Christ, but we were eyewitnesses of His greatness. For He received from God the Father honor and glory, the voice coming down to Him from the excellent glory: 'This is my beloved Son, in whom I am well pleased. Hear ye Him.' And we heard this voice brought from Heaven when we were with Him in the holy mount."[55]

Moreover, on several occasions Jesus Christ called God His Father, and Himself the Son of God. The apostles and holy Fathers reckoned this among the articles of Faith, saying, *And (I believe) in Jesus Christ, His* (i.e., God's) *only Son.*

[55] 2 Pet. 1:16-18.

2. Heresies regarding this doctrine. However, there were heretics who believed this in a distorted sense:

a. Photinus asserted that Christ is the Son of God in the same way as any other good men, who by leading a good life, merit to be called God's sons by adoption through doing God's will. Thus Christ, who led a good life and did the will of God, merited to be called a Son of God. Photinus held, in fact, that Christ did not exist before the Blessed Virgin, and that He began to exist when He was conceived of her. Thus he erred in two ways: first, by denying that Christ was the Son of God by nature; and second by asserting that with regard to His whole being, Christ began to exist in time. Our Faith, however, holds that Christ is the Son of God by nature, and that He is from eternity.

Now, Holy Scripture explicitly contradicts Photinus on both counts. Against the first it states not only that Christ is the Son, but also that He is the only-begotten Son: "The only-begotten Son who is in the bosom of the Father, He hath declared Him."[56] Against the second it states: "Before Abraham was, I am"[57] (and it is undeniable that Abraham existed before the Blessed Virgin). For this reason, against the first error the holy Fathers added in another Creed,[58] *the only Son of God;* and against the second, *eternally begotten of the Father.*

b. Sabellius, although he said that Christ was before the Blessed Virgin, denied the distinction between the Person of the Father and the Person of the Son. He said that the

[56] John 1:18.
[57] John 8:58.
[58] The Nicene Creed.

Father Himself became incarnate, so that the Person of the Father is the same as that of Christ. But this is erroneous, since it removes the Trinity of Persons, contrary to the words of John 8:16: "I am not alone, but I and the Father who sent me." It is plain that no one is sent by himself. Accordingly Sabellius lied, and therefore in the [Nicene] Creed of the Fathers, was added *God from God, Light from Light*. In other words, we must believe in God who is the Son of God the Father, and in God the Son, who is the Light of the Father who is Light.

c. Arius, while admitting that Christ was before the Blessed Virgin and that the Person of the Father was distinct from that of the Son, nevertheless attributed to Christ three things: first, that the Son of God is a creature; second, that He is the highest of all creatures made by God, not from eternity but in the course of time; and third, that God the Son was not of the same nature as God the Father, and that therefore He was not truly God.

But this again is erroneous and contrary to the authority of Holy Scripture. For it is said: "I and the Father are one"[59] (i.e., one in nature). Consequently, as the Father always was, so also was the Son; and as the Father is true God, so also is the Son. Accordingly, whereas Arius asserted that Christ was a creature, it is said by the Fathers in the [Nicene] Creed, *true God from true God*. And whereas he said that Christ was not from eternity but from time, on the contrary it is said in the [Nicene] Creed, *begotten not made*. And against his assertion that Christ was not of the same nature as the Father, it was added in the [Nicene] Creed, *one in being with the Father*.

[59] John 10:30.

25

It is clear, then, that we must believe that Christ is the only-begotten of God and the true Son of God; that He has always existed together with the Father; that the Person of the Son is distinct from the Person of the Father; and that He is of one nature with the Father. This, however, in the present life we believe by faith, but we shall know it by perfect vision in eternal life. Accordingly for our own consolation we shall make a few observations on this point.

B. Christ is the Word of God

1. How this may be understood. We must observe, then, that various things have various ways of generating. In God, generation is different from the generation of other things, so we cannot obtain a notion of divine generation except through the generation of that creature which approaches nearest to a likeness to God. Now, as we have stated, nothing is so like God as the human soul. And the manner of generation in the soul is that a man by his soul conceives something which is called the concept of the mind. This concept proceeds from the soul as from its father, and is called the word of the mind or of man. Accordingly the soul by thought generates its word.

Thus the Son of God is nothing else but the Word of God, not like the word that is uttered externally (for this is transitory) but as the word conceived inwardly. Therefore this same Word of God is of one nature with God and equal to God.

Thus in speaking of the Word of God, St. John destroys three heresies: first, the heresy of Photinus, when John says, "In the beginning was the Word"; second, that of Sabellius, when he says, "and the Word was with God"; and third, that of Arius, when he says, "and the Word was God."[60]

[60] John 1:1.

Now, a word is not in us in the same way as it is in God. In us our own word is accidental;[61] but in Him, the Word of God is the same as God Himself, since there is nothing in God that is not the divine essence. Yet no one can say that God has not a Word, for it would follow that God is most foolish.

Therefore, just as God always was, so also His Word always was. Even as a craftsman makes all things by means of the form or word which he has preconceived in his mind, so, too, God makes all things by His Word as by His art: "All things were made by Him."[62]

2. How we ought to respond to God's words. If, then, God's Word is His Son, and all His words bear a certain likeness to that Word:

> **a. We ought to be willing to hear God's words,** for it is a sign that we love God if we willingly hear His words.

> **b. We ought also to believe God's words,** since thereby the Word of God (i.e., Christ, who is God's Word) dwells in us, or to quote the Apostle: "That Christ may dwell in your hearts by faith."[63] And: "You have not His word abiding in you."[64]

> **c. The Word of God abiding in us should be continually in our thoughts,** since not only should we believe in Him, but also meditate upon Him; otherwise we would derive no profit from His presence. In fact, meditation of this kind is of great assistance against sin: "In my heart I have hidden Thy

[61] *Accidental* in this context means "not of the essence."

[62] John 1:3.

[63] Eph. 3:17.

[64] John 5:38.

27

words that I may not sin against Thee."[65] Again, it is said of the just man, "Day and night he shall meditate on His law."[66] And it is said of the Blessed Virgin that she "kept all these words, pondering on them in her heart."[67]

d. We ought to communicate God's Word to others by admonishing them, preaching to them, and inflaming their hearts. Thus the Apostle wrote to the Ephesians, "Let no evil speech proceed from your mouth, but that which is good unto edification."[68] And to the Colossians, "Let the word of Christ dwell in you abundantly: in all wisdom teaching and admonishing one another."[69] And to Timothy, "Preach the word, be insistent in season and out of season, reprove, entreat, rebuke in all patience and doctrine."[70]

e. We ought to put God's words into practice: "Be ye doers of the word and not hearers only, deceiving yourselves."[71]

3. The Virgin Mary responded to God in all of these ways. These five precepts were observed by the Blessed Virgin in their order when she begot the Word of God. First she *heard:* "The Holy Spirit shall come upon thee."[72] Then she *consented* by faith: "Behold the handmaid of the Lord."[73] Third, she *held and*

---

[65] Ps. 118:11 (RSV = Ps. 119:11).
[66] Ps. 1:2.
[67] Luke 2:19.
[68] Eph. 4:29.
[69] Col. 3:16.
[70] 2 Tim. 4:2.
[71] James 1:22.
[72] Luke 1:35.
[73] Luke 1:38.

bore Him in her womb. Fourth, she *brought Him forth* and gave birth to Him. Fifth, she *nourished and fed Him*. Hence the Church sings, "The Virgin alone gave her Heaven-filled breast to the King of angels."[74]

---

[74] Fourth Responsory, Office of the Circumcision, *Dominican Breviary*.

III

HE WAS CONCEIVED BY THE HOLY SPIRIT
AND BORN OF THE VIRGIN MARY

As we have shown, a Christian must believe not only that Christ is the Son of God, but also that He became man. Thus, St. John, having said many subtle things about the Word of God that are hard to understand,[75] goes on to tell us of the Incarnation, saying, "And the Word was made flesh."[76]

A. Analogies by which to understand the Incarnation
In order to throw some light on this subject, I shall illustrate it by means of two examples.

    1. The spoken word. In the first place, without doubt, nothing is more like the Word of God than the unvoiced word that is conceived in man's heart. Now, the word conceived in the heart is unknown to all except the one who conceives it; it is first known to others when the voice gives utterance to it. Thus the Word of God while yet in the bosom of the Father was known to the Father alone; but when He was clothed with flesh as a word is clothed with the voice, then He was first made

---

[75] John 1:1-13.
[76] John 1:14.

31

manifest and known: "Afterwards He was seen on earth and conversed with men."[77]

2. The written word. Another example lies in the fact that although the voiced word is known through hearing, it is not seen or touched; but when it is written, it is both seen and touched. In like manner, the Word of God became both visible and tangible when He was, as it were, written on our flesh.

Just as the parchment on which the king's word is written is called the king's word, so the man united to God's Word in unity of person is called the Word of God: "Take thee a great book and write in it with a man's pen."[78] And therefore the holy Apostles said, *Who was conceived by the Holy Spirit and born of the Virgin Mary.*

B. Errors regarding the Incarnation
On this point there arose many errors, which is why the holy Fathers at the Council of Nicea made several additions in another Creed[79] whereby all these errors stand condemned.

1. Origen said that Christ was born and came into the world in order to save the demons also, and so he asserted that all the demons would be saved at the end of the world. But this is contrary to Holy Scripture, for it is said: "Depart from me, ye cursed, into everlasting fire that was prepared for the Devil and his angels."[80] Therefore, in order to exclude this, the following clause was added: *For us men* (not for the demons) *and for our salvation,* thus stressing God's love for us.

---

[77] Bar. 3:38.
[78] Isa. 8:1.
[79] The Nicene Creed.
[80] Matt. 25:41.

2. Photinus admitted that Christ was born of the Virgin Mary, but asserted that He was a mere man, who by leading a good life and doing God's will, merited to become a son of God, even as other holy men. And against this it is said: "I came down from Heaven, not to do my will, but the will of Him who sent me."[81] Now it goes without saying that He would not have come down from there unless He had been there, and if He were a mere man He would not have been in Heaven. Therefore, in order to exclude this, the following words were added: *He came down from Heaven.*

3. The Manicheans said that although the Son of God always existed, and came down from Heaven, yet He had flesh not really but only apparently. But this is false, since it was unbecoming for the Teacher of truth to have anything false about Him. Therefore since He had flesh ostensibly, He really had it. Thus it is said: "Handle and see; for a spirit hath not flesh and bones, as you see me to have."[82] Therefore, in order to exclude this, they added, *And He took flesh.*[83]

4. Ebion,[84] who was of Jewish nationality, said that Christ was born of the Blessed Virgin from sexual intercourse and fecundation by the male seed. But this is false, since the angel said, "For that which is conceived in her is of the Holy Spirit."[85] Therefore the holy Fathers excluded this by adding, *By the power of the Holy Spirit.*

---

[81] John 6:38.

[82] Luke 24:39.

[83] Currently this is translated: *And became man.*

[84] The Ebionites were a sect whose doctrines were a mixture of Gnosticism and Judaism.

[85] Matt. 1:20.

33

5. Valentine, while confessing that Christ was conceived by the Holy Spirit, taught that the Holy Spirit fashioned a heavenly body which He placed in the Virgin's womb; this was Christ's body. Thus the Blessed Virgin's cooperation was reduced to her serving as a place for Christ's body. Hence Valentine said that Christ's body passed through the Blessed Virgin as through a channel.

But this is false, because the Angel said, "The Holy One that shall be born of thee shall be called the Son of God."[86] And the Apostle says, "When the fullness of time came, God sent His Son made of a woman."[87] For this reason they added, *Born of the Virgin Mary.*

6. Arius and Apollinarius said that though Christ was the Word of God born of the Virgin Mary, He had no soul but the Godhead in lieu thereof. But this is contrary to Scripture, for Christ said, "Now is my soul troubled"[88] and "My soul is sorrowful even unto death."[89] The holy Fathers excluded this by adding, *And became man,* because a man is composed of a soul and a body. So Christ had whatever a man can have, except sin.

7. Eutyches. In that He is said to have become man, all the aforesaid errors stand condemned, as well as all possible errors, especially that of Eutyches, who maintained that the divine and human natures were mixed together so as to form one nature in Christ that is neither purely divine nor purely human. This is false, since in that case He would not be a man, and this would be contrary to the words, *And became man.*

[86] Luke 1:35.
[87] Gal. 4:4.
[88] John 12:27.
[89] Matt. 26:38.

8. Nestorius. The error of Nestorius also stands condemned, for he said that the Son of God was united to man solely by indwelling. But this is false, because then He would not *be* a man, but *in* a man. That He became man is declared by the Apostle: "He was in habit found as a man."[90] "Ye seek to kill me, a man who has spoken the truth to you, which I have heard of God."[91]

C. Benefits of belief in the Incarnation
From what has been said we may gather a few points for our instruction:

1. Our faith is strengthened. For instance, if anyone were to tell us about a distant country which he had never visited, we would not believe him to the same extent as if he had been there. Accordingly, before Christ came into the world, the patriarchs, prophets, and John the Baptist said certain things about God, but men did not believe them as they believe Christ, who was with God, who indeed was one with God. For this reason our faith is very strong, seeing that we have received it from Christ: "No man has ever seen God; the only-begotten Son, who is in the bosom of the Father, He hath declared Him."[92] So it is that many mysteries of Faith have been made known to us after the coming of Christ, which until then were hidden.

2. Our hope is raised, because it is evident that God's Son took our flesh and came to us not for a trifling reason, but for our exceedingly great good. He bound Himself to us, as it were, by deigning to take a human soul and body and to be born of a

[90] Phil. 2:7.
[91] Cf. John 8:40.
[92] John 1:18.

Virgin, in order to bestow His Godhead on us. Thus He became man that man might become God: "By whom we have access through faith into this grace wherein we stand; and glory in the hope of the glory of the sons of God."[93]

3. Our charity is inflamed, because there is no greater proof of God's love than that God the Creator became a creature, that our Lord became our Brother, and that the Son of God became the Son of man: "God so loved the world that He gave His only-begotten son."[94] The very thought of this should kindle and inflame our hearts with the love of God.

4. We are encouraged to keep our souls pure, because our nature was ennobled and raised through being united to God, to the extent of being assumed into union with a divine Person. Thus after the Incarnation the angel would not allow St. John to worship him,[95] whereas an angel had suffered this from even the greatest patriarchs.[96] Consequently, man ought to bear this exaltation in mind, and in consideration of it should disdain to debase himself and his nature by falling into sin. For this reason St. Peter says, "By whom He hast given us most great and precious promises; that by these you may be made partakers of the divine nature, flying the corruption of that concupiscence which is in the world."[97]

5. Our desire to go to Christ is inflamed. For a man whose brother is king in a far distant country will have a great longing

---

[93] Rom. 5:2.
[94] John 3:16.
[95] Rev. 22:8, 9.
[96] Cf. Gen. 18:2; 19:1-2.
[97] 2 Pet. 1:4.

to go to him, to be with and stay with him. Thus, seeing that Christ is our brother, we should long to be with Him and to be united to Him: "Wheresoever the body is, there will the eagles be gathered together."[98] The Apostle also desired "to be dissolved and to be with Christ."[99] This same desire increases in us when we meditate on Christ's Incarnation.

[98] Matt. 24:28.
[99] Phil. 1:23.

IV

HE SUFFERED UNDER PONTIUS PILATE,
WAS CRUCIFIED, DIED, AND WAS BURIED

A. Christ's death is difficult to conceive
Just as a Christian is required to believe in the Incarnation of the
Son of God, so is it necessary that he believe in His Passion and
death, because as St. Augustine says, "His birth would have profited us nothing had we not profited by His Redemption."

That Christ did indeed die for us is so hard to conceive that
scarcely is our mind able to grasp it; in fact it is utterly beyond our
understanding. The Apostle insinuates this when he says, "I work a
work in your days, a work which you will not believe if any man
shall tell it to you."[100] In fact, so great is God's favor and love in our
regard that He has done more for us than we are able to understand.
However, we are not to believe that Christ suffered death in such a
way that His Godhead died, but that His human nature died; for
He died not as God, but as man. This may be illustrated by
examples.

1. The analogy in ourselves. It is clear that when a man dies, it
is not the soul, but the body or the flesh that dies when body and
soul are separated. Accordingly when Christ died, it was not
His Godhead that died, but His human nature. But surely if the

[100] Acts 13:41 (quoting Hab. 1:5).

39

Jews who opposed Christ did not kill His Godhead, they sinned no more than if they had killed any other man.

I reply that a man who bespatters a king's robe is as guilty as though he had bespattered the king himself. Hence the Jews who opposed Christ, though they could not slay God, yet for slaying the human nature wherewith Christ was clothed, were punished as though they had slain the Godhead.

2. The analogy of a king's parchment. As we have said above, the Son of God is the Word of God, and the Word of God was made flesh even as the king's word is inscribed on parchment. If, then, one were to tear the king's parchment, he would be held as guilty as if he had torn the king's word. Hence the Jews who opposed Christ are held to be as guilty as if they had slain the Word of God.

B. Why Christ suffered for us

But what need was there for the Word of God to suffer for us? That the need was great may be assigned to two reasons. One was the need for a remedy for sin; the other was the need for an example of what we ought to do.

1. Christ's passion remedies the evils incurred through sin. We find a remedy inasmuch as Christ's Passion proves a remedy for all the evils that we incur through sin. These evils are of five kinds:

a. The stain of sin. For when a man sins, he defiles his soul. Just as virtue is the soul's beauty, so is sin its stain: "How happeneth it, O Israel, that thou art in thy enemies' land? . . . Thou art defiled with the dead."[101] This is removed by Christ's

[101] Cf. Bar. 3:10, 11.

Passion, for Christ by His Passion poured out His blood as a laver in which sinners are cleansed. "He hath washed us from our sins in His own blood."[102] Now, the soul is cleansed by Christ's blood in Baptism, which from Christ's blood derives the power of regeneration. Consequently, when a man defiles himself with sin, he does an injury to Christ, and sins more grievously than before he was baptized: "A man making void the law of Moses dieth without any mercy under two or three witnesses; how much more, think you, he deserveth worse punishments who hath trodden underfoot the Son of God and hath esteemed the blood of the testament unclean?"[103]

b. The anger of God. For just as a carnal man loves carnal beauty, so does God love spiritual beauty, which is that of the soul. When, therefore, the soul is defiled by sin, God is offended and the sinner becomes an object of His hatred: "To God the wicked and his wickedness are hateful."[104] But Christ's Passion removes this, because He atoned to God the Father for sin, for which man himself was unable to atone. Christ's charity and obedience were greater than the sin and disobedience of the first man: "When we were enemies we were reconciled to God by the death of His Son."[105]

c. Weakness, which we incur because a man thinks that if he sins once he will be able afterward to refrain from sinning, whereas it is quite the reverse that happens. For by the first sin he is weakened and is more inclined to sin again;

---

[102] Apoc. 1:5 (RSV = Rev. 1:5).
[103] Heb. 10:28, 29.
[104] Wisd. 14:9.
[105] Rom. 5:10.

41

also sin has a greater power over him. Moreover, so far as he is concerned, he puts himself in a state from which there is no escape — like a man who jumps into a well — except by the power of God. So after man had sinned, our nature was weakened and corrupted, and thus man was more prone to sin.

But Christ diminished this weakness and infirmity, although He did not remove it altogether. And yet man is so strengthened and sin is so weakened by Christ's Passion, that sin has no longer such power over him. Man, by the help of God's grace bestowed in the Sacraments, which derive their efficacy from Christ's Passion, is able to endeavor to arise from his sins. Thus says the Apostle, "Our old man is crucified with Him, that the body of sin may be destroyed."[106] For before Christ's Passion there were few who lived without falling into mortal sin, whereas afterward many have lived and are living without mortal sin.

d. The debt of punishment, which we incur because God's justice demands that whoever sins should be punished. Now, punishment is awarded according to guilt. Thus, since the guilt of mortal sin is infinite, being against the infinite good (namely, God) whose commandments the sinner holds in contempt, it follows that the punishment due to mortal sin is infinite.

But Christ by His Passion delivered us from this punishment which He bore Himself: "He bore our sins in His body"[107] (i.e., the punishment due to our sins). For His Passion was so efficacious that it suffices to atone for all the sins of the whole world, even of a hundred thousand worlds. For

[106] Rom. 6:6.
[107] 1 Pet. 2:24.

this reason when a man is baptized he is released from all his sins; so also it is that a priest forgives sins; and again that the more a man conforms to the Passion of Christ, the more is he pardoned and the more grace he merits.

e. Banishment from the kingdom. Those who offend their king are compelled to leave the kingdom, and thus on account of sin man is banished from Paradise. For this reason, immediately after he had sinned Adam was banished from Paradise and the gates of Eden were closed.

But Christ by His Passion opened the gates and recalled the exiles to the kingdom. For when Christ's side was pierced, the gates of Paradise were opened, and by the shedding of His blood the stain of sin was wiped away, God was appeased, man's weakness was removed, his punishment was expiated, and the exiles were called back to the kingdom. Hence the thief received the immediate response, "This day shalt thou be with me in Paradise."[108] This had not been said of old — not to Adam, not to Abraham, not to David. But "this day" (i.e., as soon as the gates were opened) the thief having sought pardon, found it: "Having . . . confidence in the entering into the holies by the blood of Christ."[109]

2. Christ's passion as a model of virtues. Accordingly it is clear how profitable was Christ's Passion as a remedy, but it is not less profitable as an example. For as St. Augustine says, Christ's Passion affords us a model in all the circumstances of life, since whoever wishes to lead a perfect life needs only to despise what Christ despised on the Cross and to desire what He desired.

[108] Luke 23:43.
[109] Heb. 10:19.

There is no virtue an example of which we do not find on the Cross.

a. Charity. If you seek an example of charity, "greater love hath no man than that he lays down his life for his friends,"[110] and this Christ did on the Cross. If He laid down His life for us, we should not deem it a hardship to suffer any evils whatever for His sake: "What shall I render unto the Lord for all the things which He hath rendered to me?"[111]

b. Patience. If you seek an example of patience, you will find a most perfect example on the Cross. For a man's patience is proved to be great on two counts: either when he suffers great evils patiently or when he suffers that which he is able to avoid yet does not avoid.

Now, Christ suffered greatly on the Cross: "O all ye that pass by the way, attend and see if there be any sorrow like unto my sorrow."[112] And He suffered patiently inasmuch as "when He suffered He threatened not."[113] "He shall be led as a sheep to the slaughter, and shall be dumb as a lamb before His shearer."[114]

Moreover He could have escaped but did not escape: "Thinkest thou that I cannot ask my Father and He will give me presently more than twelve legions of angels?"[115] Great therefore was Christ's patience on the Cross: "Let us run by patience to the fight proposed to us; looking on Jesus the

[110] John 15:13.
[111] Ps. 115:12 (RSV = Ps. 116:12).
[112] Lam. 1:12.
[113] 1 Pet. 2:23.
[114] Isa. 53:7.
[115] Matt. 26:53.

author and finisher of faith who, having joy set before Him, endured the Cross, despising the shame."[116]

c. Humility. If you seek an example of humility, look on the Crucified. Although He was God, He chose to be judged by Pontius Pilate and to suffer death: "Thy cause hath been judged as that of the wicked."[117] Truly *as that of the wicked* because: "Let us condemn Him to a most shameful death."[118] The Master chose to die for His servant; the Life of the Angels suffered death for man: "Made obedient unto death."[119]

d. Obedience. If you seek an example of obedience, follow Him who was made obedient to the Father even unto death: "As by the disobedience of one man, many were made sinners, so also by the obedience of one, many shall be made just."[120]

e. Contempt for earthly things. If you seek an example of contempt for earthly things, follow Him, the King of kings and Lord of lords, in whom are the treasures of wisdom; and see Him on the Cross — despoiled, derided, spat upon, scourged, crowned with thorns, served with gall and hyssop, dead. Therefore, take no account of your apparel or possessions, since "they parted my garments amongst them;"[121] nor of honors, since I suffered myself to be jeered at and scourged; nor of rank, since they plaited a crown of thorns and placed

[116] Heb. 12:1, 2.
[117] Job 36:17.
[118] Wisd. 2:20.
[119] Cf. Phil. 2:8.
[120] Rom. 5:19.
[121] Ps. 21:19 (RSV = Ps. 22:18).

it on my head; nor of pleasures, since "in my thirst they gave me vinegar to drink."[122] Thus St. Augustine in commenting on Heb. 12:2 ("who, having joy set before Him, endured the Cross, despising the shame") says, "Christ the man despised all earthly things in order to teach us to despise them."

---

[122] Ps. 68:22 (RSV = Ps. 69:21).

V

HE DESCENDED INTO HELL

As we have stated, Christ's death, like that of other men, consisted in the separation of His soul from His body. But His Godhead was so inseparably united to the man Christ that although His soul and body were separated from each other, His Godhead always remained most perfectly united to both His soul and His body. Consequently, in the tomb there was His body, together with the Son of God, who together with His soul descended into Hell.

A. Reasons for Christ's descent into Hell

There are four reasons why Christ, together with His soul, descended into Hell:

1. **That He might bear the whole punishment of sin,** so that He might wholly atone for sin. Now, the punishment of man's sin was not only the death of the body. There was also a punishment in the soul, for seeing that sin had been committed in the soul, the soul was punished by being deprived of the Beatific Vision and as yet no atonement had been offered for the abolishment of this punishment. For this reason, after their death and before the coming of Christ, all, even the holy patriarchs, went down into Hell.

So in order to bear the entire punishment due to sinners, Christ chose not only to die but also that His soul should descend into Hell. Thus it is said: "I am counted among them that go down into the pit. I am become as a man without help, free among the dead."[123] For others were there under constraint, whereas Christ was there as free.

2. That He might bring perfect succor to all His friends. For He had His friends not only in the world but also in Hell, since one is Christ's friend by having charity and in Hell there were many who had died in charity and faith in Christ to come, such as Abraham, Isaac, Jacob, Moses, David, and other righteous and perfect men. And since Christ had visited His friends in the world and had succored them by His death, He wished to visit His friends who were in Hell and succor them by coming to them: "I will penetrate to all the lower parts of the earth, and will behold all that sleep, and will enlighten all that hope in the Lord."[124]

3. That He might completely overcome the Devil, since a man's triumph over another is complete when he conquers him not only in the open field, but attacks him in his stronghold and deprives him of his kingdom and even of his dwelling place. Now, Christ had triumphed over the Devil[125] and had conquered him on the Cross. Thus He said: "Now is the judgment of the world; now shall the prince of this world" (i.e., the Devil) "be cast out."[126] And, therefore, that His victory might be complete, it was His will to deprive the Devil of his throne and imprison him in his own house, which is Hell. For this reason He descended into Hell, deprived the Devil of his own, bound him,

---

[123] Ps. 87:5 (RSV = Ps. 88:4-5).

[124] Ecclus. 24:45 (No equivalent in RSV).

[125] When He was tempted in the desert.

[126] John 12:31.

and carried off his spoils: "Despoiling the principalities and powers, He hath exposed them confidently, openly triumphing over them in himself."[127]

Moreover, since Christ had been given power and possession in Heaven and on earth, He wished to take possession of Hell, so that, to quote the Apostle, "In the name of Jesus every knee should bow of those that are in Heaven, on earth, and under the earth."[128] "In my name they shall cast out devils."[129]

4. To deliver the saints who were in Hell. For just as Christ wished to suffer death that He might deliver the living from death, so did He wish to descend into Hell in order to deliver those that were there: "Thou also by the blood of thy testament hath sent forth thy prisoners out of the pit wherein is no water."[130] "O death, I will be thy death; O Hell, I will be thy bite.[131]

For although Christ destroyed death altogether, He did not altogether destroy Hell, but took a piece out of it, as it were, in that He did not deliver all who were there, but only those who were free from mortal sin as well as Original Sin. As regards the latter, they were freed personally therefrom by circumcision or before circumcision — either (in the case of those who died before having the use of reason) by the faith of their parents who were believers or (in the case of adults) by sacrifices and their faith in Christ to come.

Yet all these were in Hell as having contracted Original Sin from Adam, from which, as members of the human race, they

---

[127] Col. 2:15.
[128] Phil. 2:10.
[129] Mark 16:17.
[130] Zach. 9:11.
[131] Osee 13:14 (RSV = Hos. 13:14).

could not be freed except by Christ. Therefore, He left there those who had gone down there with the stain of mortal sin as well as the uncircumcised children; and in this sense He said, "O Hell, I will be thy bite." Thus we know that Christ descended into Hell, and why.

B. What we may learn from Christ's descent into Hell
From this exposition, there are four points we may gather for our instruction.

1. A firm hope in God, because no matter how great a man's afflictions may be, he should always hope in God's assistance and trust in Him. Nothing is so grievous as to be in Hell. So if Christ freed those who were in Hell, anyone — provided he is a friend of God — should be confident that God will deliver him from his straits whatever they are: "She [wisdom] forsook not the just when he was sold . . . and went down with him into the pit, and in bands she left him not."[132] And seeing that God gives special assistance to His servants, anyone who serves God should be full of confidence: "He that feareth the Lord shall tremble at nothing; he shall not be afraid, for He is his hope."[133]

2. We ought to conceive fear and cast away presumption. For although Christ suffered for sinners and descended into Hell, yet He did not deliver all, but only those who were free from mortal sin (as we have said) whereas He left those who had died in mortal sin. Consequently, no one who goes down to Hell in a state of mortal sin may hope for pardon, but he will remain in Hell as long as the holy Fathers remain in Paradise, i.e., for all

[132] Wisd. 10:13, 14.
[133] Ecclus. 34:16 (RSV = Sir. 34:14).

eternity: "These shall go into everlasting punishment: but the just into life everlasting."[134]

3. We should bear this in mind. For as Christ descended into Hell for our salvation, so we ought to take care to descend there by considering its punishments, even as did the saintly Hezekiah: "I said: In the midst of my days I shall go to the gates of Hell."[135] For anyone who in thought frequently goes down to Hell in life, is not likely to go down there in death, because such thoughts withdraw us from sin.

Thus we observe that the people of this world are wary of evil-doing for fear of temporal punishment. How much more, then, should they be wary for fear of the punishment of Hell, which is greater both in respect to its severity and in respect to its manifold nature: "Remember thy last end, and thou shalt never sin."[136]

4. We may gather an example of love. Christ descended into Hell in order to deliver His own. So, too, we ought to descend there in order to succor our friends, inasmuch as they are helpless. Therefore we ought to succor those who are in Purgatory. Surely he would be very cruel who would not succor his friend in an earthly prison; much more cruel, then, is he who does not succor his friend in Purgatory, since there is no comparison between the world's punishments and those of Purgatory: "Have pity on me, have pity on me, at least you my friends, for the hand of the Lord hath touched me."[137] "It is a holy and wholesome thought to pray for the dead that they be loosed from

[134] Matt. 25:46.
[135] Isa. 38:10.
[136] Ecclus. 7:40 (RSV = Sir. 7:36).
[137] Job 19:21.

sins."[138] According to St. Augustine, this succor is given to them under three forms: by Masses, by prayers, and by almsgiving. And Gregory adds a fourth: fasting. And it is no wonder, seeing that even in this world one friend can pay a debt for another (but this applies only to those who are in Purgatory).

[138] 2 Macc. 12:46.

VI

ON THE THIRD DAY HE ROSE AGAIN
FROM THE DEAD

A. Christ rose from the dead in order to teach us

Man needs to know two things: the glory of God and the punishment of Hell. For through being drawn by His glory and terrified by His punishments, men are careful on their own account and refrain from sin. Yet these things are very difficult for a man to know. As is said of God's glory, "who shall search out the things that are in Heaven?"[139] This, however, is difficult to the earthly-minded because "he that is of the earth . . . speaketh of the earth," whereas it is not difficult for the spiritual man, because "he that cometh from Heaven is above all."[140] Hence God came down from Heaven and took flesh in order to teach us heavenly things.

It was also difficult to know about the punishments of Hell, for "no man hath been known to have returned from Hell,"[141] which is said in the person of the wicked. But it cannot be said now, since just as He came down from Heaven in order to teach us heavenly things, so did He come back from Hell in order to teach us about Hell. Consequently, we must believe not only that He became man and died, but also that He rose again from the dead. And

[139] Wisd. 9:16.
[140] John 3:31.
[141] Wisd. 2:1.

therefore the Creed goes on: *On the third day, He rose again from the dead.*

B. Christ's Resurrection differs from that of others

Now, as we are aware, there were several who rose from the dead, namely, Lazarus,[142] the widow's son,[143] and the daughter of the ruler of the synagogue.[144] But Christ's Resurrection differs from the resurrection of these and of others in four respects.

1. They differ in the cause of their resurrection, in that others who came back to life arose not by their own power but either by Christ's power or at the prayer of a saint, whereas Christ arose by His own power. For He was not only man but God, and the Godhead of the Word was never separated either from His soul or from His body. Therefore, whenever He chose, His body could resume His soul and His soul could resume His body: "I have power to lay down my life, and I have power to take it up again."[145]

And although He died, it was neither through weakness nor of necessity, but through power, since He chose to die. This is evident from the fact that in the moment of dying He cried out with a loud voice,[146] which others cannot do at the moment of death, for they die from weakness. For this reason, the centurion exclaimed, "Verily this was the Son of God."[147] Therefore, just as by His own power He laid down His life, so by His own power He took it up again. For this reason it is said, *He rose*

[142] John 11:1-44.
[143] Luke 7:11-16.
[144] Mark 5:35-43.
[145] John 10:18.
[146] Matt. 27:50.
[147] Matt. 27:54.

again, and not that He was raised up as though by another: "I have slept and have taken my rest and I have risen up."[148] Nor is this contradicted by the words, "This Jesus hath God raised again,"[149] because both the Father and the Son raised Him up, since the Father's power is one and the same as the Son's.

2. They differ in the life to which each rose again, for Christ arose to a glorious and incorruptible life: "Christ is risen from the dead through the glory of the Father,"[150] whereas others rise again to the same life which they had before, as in the case of Lazarus and others.

3. They differ in their fruit and efficacy, for by virtue of Christ's Resurrection all rise again ("Many bodies of the saints that had slept arose"[151]), and the Apostle declares that "Christ is risen from the dead, the firstfruits of them that sleep."[152] And behold how Christ by His Passion attained glory ("Ought not Christ to have suffered these things and so to enter into His glory?"[153]) in order to teach us how we may be able to attain glory: "Through many tribulations we must enter into the kingdom of God."[154]

4. They differ with regard to time. Christ rose again on the third day, whereas the resurrection of others is deferred to the end of the world (except in special cases where some have been

---

[148] Ps. 3:6 (RSV = Ps. 3:5).
[149] Acts 2:32.
[150] Rom. 6:4.
[151] Matt. 27:52.
[152] 1 Cor. 15:20.
[153] Luke 24:26.
[154] Acts 14:21.

privileged to rise again earlier, as, for instance, the Blessed Virgin and, according to a pious tradition, St. John the Evangelist). The reason for this is that Christ's Resurrection, death, and birth were for "our salvation,"[155] and therefore He chose to rise again at such time as would be profitable for our salvation. Had He risen again at once, people would not have believed that He had died, and if He had delayed His resurrection for a long time, His disciples would not have remained faithful, and consequently His Passion would have profited no one: "What profit is there in my blood whilst I go down to corruption?"[156] For this reason, He rose again the third day, that it might be believed that He died and that the disciples might not lose faith in Him.

C. What Christ's Resurrection teaches us
From the above we may gather four points for our instruction:

1. We should strive to rise again spiritually from the death of the soul which we incur by sin, to the life of righteousness which becomes ours by repentance. Thus the Apostle says, "Rise, thou that sleepest, and arise from the dead, and Christ shall enlighten thee."[157] This is the first resurrection: "Blessed . . . is he that hath part in the first resurrection."[158]

2. We should not delay rising again until the time of death, but should do so quickly, seeing that Christ rose again on the third day: "Delay not to be converted to the Lord, and defer it not from day to day."[159] For when you are burdened with sickness,

[155] The Nicene Creed.
[156] Ps. 29:10 (RSV = Ps. 30:9).
[157] Eph. 5:14.
[158] Apoc. 20:6 (RSV = Rev. 20:6).
[159] Ecclus. 5:8 (RSV = Sir. 5:7).

you will be unable to think of those things which concern your salvation, and also because by persisting in sin you forfeit a share in all the good works that are done in the Church, besides incurring many evils. Moreover, the longer the Devil possesses us, as Bede says, the more loath he is to lose his hold on us.

3. We should rise again to an incorruptible life. In other words, we should rise so as not to die again, through having the resolve not to sin again: "Christ rising from the dead dieth now no more; death shall no more have dominion over Him. . . . So do you also reckon that you are dead to sin, but alive unto God, in Christ Jesus our Lord. Let not sin therefore reign in your mortal body, so as to obey the lusts thereof; neither yield ye your mortal body, so as to obey the lusts thereof; neither yield ye your members as instruments of iniquity unto sin, but present yourselves to God as those that are alive from the dead."[160]

4. We rise to a new and glorious life by avoiding whatever was an occasion or a cause of death and sin: "As Christ is risen from the dead by the glory of the Father, so may we also walk in the newness of life."[161] This new life is the life of righteousness which renews the soul and brings us to the life of glory. *Amen.*

[160] Rom. 6:9, 10-13.
[161] Rom. 6:4.

VII

HE ASCENDED INTO HEAVEN
AND IS SEATED AT THE RIGHT HAND
OF GOD, THE FATHER ALMIGHTY

Furthermore we must believe in Christ's ascension, that He ascended into Heaven on the fortieth day after His resurrection. Hence the words, *He ascended into Heaven*. In this connection we must observe three things — namely, that Christ's Ascension was sublime, reasonable, and profitable:

A. Christ's Ascension was sublime
It was sublime, since He ascended into Heaven. This is expounded in three ways:

1. **He ascended above all the corporeal heavens:** "He . . . ascended above all the heavens."[162] This was realized first of all in Christ, since hitherto there was no earthly body except on earth. In fact, even Adam was in an earthly paradise.

2. **He ascended above all the spiritual heavens,** i.e., above spiritual natures: "Raising [Jesus] up from the dead and setting Him on His right hand in the heavenly places, above all principality, and power, and virtue, and dominion, and every name that is

[162] Eph. 4:10.

59

named, not only in this world, but also in that which is to come; and He hath subjected all things under His feet."[163]

3. He ascended even to the Father's throne: "Lo, one like the Son of man came with the clouds of Heaven; and He came even to the Ancient of days."[164] "And the Lord Jesus after He had spoken to them was taken up to Heaven and sitteth at the right hand of God."[165] *Right hand* is not to be taken literally, but metaphorically, when we speak of God. For Christ *as God* is said to sit "at the right hand of the Father," i.e, in equality with the Father, while *as man* He sits at the right hand of the Father as being next to Him in the 'mightier goods.'[166] Now, this is what the Devil craved for: "I will ascend into Heaven. I will exalt my throne above the stars. I will sit in the mountain of the covenant, in the sides of the north. I will ascend above the height of the clouds. I will be like the Most High."[167] But Christ alone arose to that height, and therefore it is said that *He ascended into Heaven and is seated at the right hand of the Father.* "The Lord said unto my Lord, 'Sit thou at my right hand.' "[168]

B. Christ's Ascension was reasonable
For three reasons, Christ's Ascension was reasonable, since it was "into Heaven":

1. Heaven was due to Christ according to His nature, for it is natural for a thing to return to the place where it originated.

---

[163] Eph. 1:20-22.
[164] Dan. 7:13.
[165] Mark 16:19.
[166] St. Thomas Aquinas, *Summa Theologica*, III, Q. 58, art. 3.
[167] Isa. 14:13, 14.
[168] Ps. 109:1 (RSV = Ps. 110:1).

Now, Christ drew His origin from God who is above all: "I came forth from the Father, and am come into the world; again I leave the world and I go to the Father."[169] "No man hath ascended into Heaven but He that descended from Heaven, the Son of man who is in Heaven."[170] And though the saints ascend to Heaven, they do not do so as Christ did, because Christ ascended by His own power, whereas the saints are drawn up by Christ: "Draw me after Thee."[171] Or it may be said that no man but Christ has ascended into Heaven, because the saints do not ascend there except as members of Christ, who is the head of the Church: "Wheresoever the body shall be, there shall the eagles be gathered together."[172]

2. Heaven was due to Christ because of His victory, for He was sent into the world in order to fight the Devil and He overcame him, which is why He merited to be exalted above all things: "I have overcome and am set down with my Father on His throne."[173]

3. It was reasonable on account of His humility. There never was humility so great as that of Christ, who although He was God, chose to become man; and who, although He was Lord, chose to take the form of a servant, being made obedient unto death,[174] and descended into the depths of Hell. Therefore He merited to be exalted to the heights of Heaven, to the very throne of God, because humility is the road to exaltation: "He

---

[169] John 16:28.
[170] John 3:13.
[171] *Vulg.*, "Draw me: we will run after Thee" (Cant. 1:3).
[172] Matt. 24:28.
[173] Apoc. 3:21 (RSV = Rev. 3:21).
[174] Phil. 2:8.

that humbleth himself shall be exalted."[175] "He that descended is the same also who ascended above all the Heavens."[176]

C. Christ's Ascension was profitable

In three ways, Christ's ascension was profitable:

1. As He is our leader, inasmuch as He ascended in order to lead us there, because we knew not the way but He showed it to us: "He shall go up that shall open the way before them."[177] And he ascended in order to assure us of possession of the Heavenly kingdom: "I go to prepare a place for you."[178]

2. To increase our confidence in Him, for He ascended in order to intercede for us: "He is able . . . to save . . . them that come to God by Him, always living to make intercession for us."[179] "We have an advocate with the Father, Jesus Christ the just."[180]

3. To draw our hearts to Him: "Wheresoever thy treasure is, there also is thy heart,"[181] so that we may despise temporal things. Hence the Apostle says, "If you be risen with Christ, seek the things that are above, where Christ is sitting at the right hand of God. Mind the things that are above, not the things that are upon the earth."[182]

[175] Luke 14:11.
[176] Eph. 4:10.
[177] Mic. 2:13.
[178] John 14:2.
[179] Heb. 7:25.
[180] 1 John 2:1.
[181] Matt. 6:21.
[182] Col. 3:1-2.

VIII

HE WILL COME AGAIN TO JUDGE
THE LIVING AND THE DEAD

A. Judgment belongs to Christ

It belongs to the office of a king and of a lord to judge: "The king that sitteth on the throne of judgment scattereth away all evil with his look."[183] Since, then, Christ ascended into Heaven and sits at the right hand of God, as Lord of all, it is evident that judgment belongs to Him. For this reason, in the rule of the Catholic Faith we confess that *He will come to judge the living and the dead.* The same is expressed in the words of the angels: "This Jesus who is taken up from you into Heaven, shall so come, as you have seen Him going into Heaven."[184]

Three points must be considered in connection with this judgment: 1) the form of the judgment, 2) that this judgment is to be feared, and 3) how we are to prepare for this judgment.

B. The form of the judgment

Regarding the form of the judgment, three points must be considered: 1) Who will judge? 2) Who will be judged? and 3) On what will they be judged?

---

[183] Prov. 20:8.
[184] Acts 1:11.

1. The judge is Christ: "It is He who was appointed by God to be the judge of the living and the dead,"[185] whether we take *the living* to signify those who live aright and *the dead* to signify sinners, or we take *the living* to mean those who literally will then be actually alive and *the dead* to mean those who literally will have died. Christ judges not only as God, but also as man, for three reasons:

a. So the judged may see their judge. Christ is the judge because those to be judged should see the judge. But the Godhead is an object of such great delight, that no one can see it without joy; thus, none of the damned will be able to see it, since then he would rejoice. Hence it is necessary that Christ appear in the form of man so as to be seen by all: "He hath given Him power to make judgment because He is the Son of man."[186]

b. He deserves to be judge. Christ is the judge because He merited this position as man. Since as man He was judged unjustly, God made Him judge over the whole world: "Thy cause hath been judged as that of the wicked; cause and judgment thou shalt recover."[187]

c. So that men might not lose all hope. Christ is the judge so that men — being judged by a man — will not lose all hope. For if God alone were judge, men would lose hope through terror: "They will see the Son of man coming in a cloud."[188]

---

[185] Acts 10:42.
[186] John 5:27.
[187] Job 36:17.
[188] Luke 21:27.

2. All will be judged (past, present, and future). Thus the Apostle says, "We must all be manifested before the judgment-seat of Christ, that everyone may receive the proper things of the body according as he hath done, whether it be good or evil."[189]

There are, as Gregory says, four different classes of those who are to be judged. First, those who are to be judged are either good or bad:

a. The wicked

1. Some will be condemned but not judged (namely, unbelievers whose works will not be discussed) since "he that believeth not is already judged."[190]

2. Some will be both condemned and judged (namely, the faithful who die in mortal sin): "The wages of sin is death."[191] Because of the faith they had, they will not be excluded from the judgment.

b. The good

1. Some will be saved and will not be judged (namely, those who for God's sake are poor in spirit). Indeed, they will judge others: "You who have followed me, in the regeneration when the Son of man shall sit on the seat of His majesty, you also shall sit on twelve seats judging the twelve tribes of Israel."[192] This refers not only to the

[189] 2 Cor. 5:10.
[190] John 3:18.
[191] Rom. 6:23.
[192] Matt. 19:28.

disciples, but also to all the poor. Otherwise Paul, who labored more than the others, would not be of their number. Consequently, we must understand these words to refer to all who follow the Apostles, and to men with an apostolic spirit. Hence the Apostle says, "Know ye not that we shall judge the angels?"[193] "The Lord will enter into judgment with the ancients of His people and its princes."[194]

2. Some will be both saved and judged (namely, those who die in a state of righteousness). For although they died righteous, yet through being occupied with temporal matters they fell somewhat, and so they will be judged yet saved.

3. They will be judged on all their works. In fact, they will be judged concerning all their works, both good and bad: "Walk in the ways of thy heart . . . and know that for all these God will bring thee into judgment."[195] "All things that are done God will bring into judgment for every error, whether it be good or evil."[196] "Every idle word that men shall speak, they shall render an account for it in the day of judgment."[197] Of thoughts it is said: "Inquisition shall be made into the thoughts of the ungodly."[198]

Thus it is clear what will be the form of judgment.

---

[193] 1 Cor. 6:3.
[194] Isa. 3:14.
[195] Eccles. 11:9.
[196] Eccles. 12:14.
[197] Matt. 12:36.
[198] Wisd. 1:9.

C. Why the judgment is to be feared
This judgment is to feared for four reasons:

1. Because of the Judge's wisdom. For He knows all — thoughts, words, and deeds — since "all things are naked and open to His eyes,"[199] and "all the ways of a man are open to His eyes."[200] He knows our words ("The ear of jealousy heareth all things"[201]) as well as our thoughts: "The heart is perverse above all things and unsearchable. Who can know it? — I, the Lord, who search the heart and prove the reins, who give to everyone according to his way and according to the fruit of his devices."[202] Moreover, the witnesses will be infallible, namely, men's own consciences: "Their conscience bearing witness to them and their thoughts between themselves accusing or also defending one another, in the day when God shall judge the secrets of men."[203]

2. Because of the Judge's power. For He is almighty in Himself ("Behold the Lord God shall come with strength"[204]) and also almighty in others ("The whole world shall fight with Him against the unwise"[205]). Hence Job said, "Whereas there is no man that can deliver out of Thy hand,"[206] and the Psalmist said, "If I ascend into Heaven Thou art there; if I descend into Hell Thou art present."[207]

[199] Heb. 4:13.
[200] Prov. 16:2.
[201] Wisd. 1:10.
[202] Jer. 17:9, 10.
[203] Rom. 2:15, 16.
[204] Isa. 40:10.
[205] Wisd. 5:21.
[206] Job 10:7.
[207] Ps. 138:8 (RSV = Ps. 139:8).

3. Because of the Judge's inflexible justice. For now is the time for mercy, whereas the time to come will be the time for justice only. Thus the present time is ours, but the future will be God's alone: "When I shall take a time I shall judge justices."[208] "The jealousy and rage of the husband will not spare in the day of revenge; nor will he yield to any man's prayers; nor will he accept for satisfaction ever so many gifts."[209]

4. Because of the Judge's anger. For to the just He will present a sweet and smiling countenance: "They shall see the king in His beauty."[210] But to the wicked He will appear angry and pitiless, so that they will say to the mountains, "Fall upon us and hide us from the . . . wrath of the Lamb."[211] This wrath of God does not imply disturbance of God's mind, but the effect of wrath, namely, the eternal punishment inflicted on sinners. Origen says, "How straitened will the ways of sinners be at the judgment; and yet over and above, the Judge will be incensed against them."

D. How we are to prepare for the judgment
There are four remedies against this fear of the judgment:

1. Good deeds. "Wilt thou then not be afraid of the power? Do that which is good; and thou shalt have praise from the same."[212]

2. Confession and repentance of the evil done. This should include three conditions: sorrow of heart, shame in confession, and rigor of satisfaction. These atone for eternal punishment.

---

[208] Ps. 74:3 (RSV = Ps. 75:2).
[209] Prov. 6:34, 35.
[210] Isa. 33:17.
[211] Apoc. 6:16 (RSV = Rev. 6:16).
[212] Rom. 13:3.

3. Almsgiving, which cleanses us from all stains: "Make unto yourselves friends of the mammon of iniquity that when you shall fail they may receive you into everlasting dwellings."[213]

4. Charity, namely, the love of God and our neighbor, for "charity covereth a multitude of sins."[214]

---

[213] Luke 16:9.
[214] Prov. 10:12; 1 Pet. 4:8.

IX

I BELIEVE IN THE HOLY SPIRIT

As we have said above, the Word of God is the Son of God, just as man's word is a concept of man's intellect. Now, man's word is sometimes a dead word; for instance, if he thinks of what he ought to do, but does not have the will to do it. Such is faith without works, in which case faith is said to be dead.[215] But God's is a living Word ("The word of God is living"[216]), and so in God besides the Word there is will and love. Hence St. Augustine says, "The Word of which we wish to speak is knowledge with love."[217] Now just as the Word of God is the Son of God, so is God's love the Holy Spirit. Consequently, a man has the Holy Spirit when he loves God: "The charity of God is poured forth in our hearts by the Holy Spirit who is given to us."[218]

Now, some, through entertaining a false opinion about the Holy Spirit, held that He is a creature, less than the Father and the Son, and that He is God's servant and minister. Therefore, in order to condemn these errors, the holy Fathers added to the second [Nicene] Creed five clauses about the Holy Spirit:

[215] James 2:17, 26.
[216] Heb. 4:12.
[217] *De Trinitate*, IX, 10.
[218] Rom. 5:5.

A. Characteristics of the Holy Spirit

1. The Lord. Although there are other spirits, namely, the angels, they are God's ministers: "Are they not all ministering spirits?"[219] But the Holy Spirit is the Lord: "God is a Spirit";[220] "The Lord is a Spirit."[221] Consequently, "where the Spirit of the Lord is, there is liberty,"[222] the reason being that He makes us love God and cease to love the world. Hence the words, *I believe in the Holy Spirit, the Lord*.

2. The Giver of Life. The soul's life is union with God, inasmuch as God is the life of the soul (just as the soul is the life of the body). Now, the Holy Spirit unites us to God by love, for He is Himself God's love, which is why He gives life: "It is the Spirit that quickeneth."[223] Hence they added, *The Giver of Life*.

3. Who proceeds from the Father and the Son. The Holy Spirit is one in being with the Father and the Son, because just as the Son is God's Word, so the Holy Spirit is the love of the Father and the Son. Consequently, He proceeds from both. And just as God's Word is one in being with the Father, even so God's Love is one in being with the Father and the Son. Hence the addition, *who proceeds from the Father and the Son*, from which it is evident that He is not a creature.

4. With the Father and the Son He is worshiped and glorified. He is to be worshiped equally with the Father and the Son:

[219] Heb. 1:14.
[220] John 4:24.
[221] 2 Cor. 3:17.
[222] Ibid.
[223] John 6:64 (RSV = John 6:63).

"True adorers shall adore the Father in spirit and in truth."[224] "Teach all nations, baptizing them in the name of the Father and of the Son and of the Holy Spirit."[225] For this reason the following clause was added: *With the Father and the Son He is worshiped and glorified.*

5. He has spoken through the prophets. This clause, by which the Holy Spirit is declared to be equal to God, states that the holy prophets spoke on behalf of God. Now, it is clear that if the Holy Spirit were not God, it could not be said that the prophets spoke on His behalf. But St. Peter states: "The holy men of God spoke, inspired by the Holy Spirit."[226] "The Lord God hath sent me, and His Spirit."[227] Therefore, we have this clause added: *He has spoken through the prophets.*

Hereby two errors stand condemned: the error of the Manicheans, who said that the Old Testament did not come from God (which is false since the Holy Spirit spoke through the prophets) and the error of Priscilla and Montanus, who maintained that the prophets spoke not on behalf of the Holy Spirit but as though they were out of their minds.

B. Fruits of the Holy Spirit
We derive many fruits from the Holy Spirit:

1. Forgiveness of sins. The Holy Spirit cleanses us from our sins. This is because a thing is repaired by the same one who made it. Now, the soul is created by the Holy Spirit because by Him God makes all things, for it is through loving His own

[224] John 4:23.
[225] Matt. 28:19.
[226] 2 Pet. 1:21.
[227] Isa. 48:16.

goodness that God is the cause of all: "Thou lovest all the things that are, and hatest none of the things that Thou hast made."[228] In this sense Dionysius says, "God's love did not allow Him to be barren."[229]

Consequently, the human heart which is ruined by sin must be restored by the Holy Spirit: "Send forth Thy Spirit and they shall be created, and Thou shalt renew the face of the earth."[230] Nor need we wonder that the Spirit cleanses, seeing that all sins are forgiven through love: "Many sins are forgiven her, because she hath loved much."[231] "Charity covereth all sins."[232] "Charity covereth a multitude of sins."[233]

2. Enlightenment. The Holy Spirit enlightens our mind, because whatever we know, it is through the Holy Spirit that we know it: "But the Holy Spirit, the Paraclete, whom the Father will send in my name, will Himself teach you all things and will bring all things to your mind, whatsoever I shall have said to you."[234] "His unction teacheth you of all things."[235]

3. Adherence to the Commandments. The Holy Spirit helps us (and to a certain extent compels us) to keep the Commandments. For no one can keep the Commandments unless he loves God: "If any man loves me, he will keep my word."[236]

---

[228] Wisd. 11:25.
[229] *Div. Nom.*, 4.
[230] Ps. 103:30 (RSV = Ps. 104:30).
[231] Luke 7:47.
[232] Prov. 10:12.
[233] 1 Pet. 4:8.
[234] John 14:26.
[235] 1 John 2:27.
[236] John 14:23.

Now, the Holy Spirit makes us love God; therefore He helps us to keep the Commandments: "I will give you a new heart, and I will put a new spirit within you; and I will take away the stony heart out of your flesh, and I will give you a heart of flesh. And I will put my spirit in the midst of you; and I will cause you to walk in my commandments and to keep my judgments and do them."[237]

4. Hope. The Holy Spirit strengthens our hope of eternal life, inasmuch as He is a kind of surety that we shall inherit it. Hence the Apostle says, "You were signed with the Holy Spirit of promise who is the pledge of our inheritance,"[238] for He is, as it were, a token of eternal life. The reason is that eternal life is due to a man inasmuch as he is made a son of God.

This is effected through his becoming like Christ; and a man becomes like Christ through having the Spirit of Christ, which is the Holy Spirit: "For you have not received the spirit of bondage again in fear, but you have received the spirit of adoption of sons whereby we cry: *Abba* ("Father"). For the Spirit himself giveth testimony to our spirit that we are the sons of God."[239] "And because you are sons, God hath sent the Spirit of His Son into your hearts crying: *Abba*, Father."[240]

5. Counsel. He counsels us when we are in doubt and teaches us what is God's will: "He that hath an ear, let him hear what the Spirit saith. . . ."[241] "That I may hear Him as a master."[242]

---

[237] Ezek. 36:26, 27.
[238] Eph. 1:13, 14.
[239] Rom. 8:15, 16.
[240] Gal. 4:6.
[241] Apoc. 2:17 (RSV = Rev. 2:17).
[242] Isa. 50:4.

X

THE HOLY CATHOLIC CHURCH

Just as one man has one soul and one body yet many members, so the Catholic Church is one body, having many members. The soul that gives life to this body is the Holy Spirit. So after confessing our belief in the Holy Spirit, we are bid to believe in the Holy Catholic Church. Hence the Creed continues, *the Holy Catholic Church*.

Here let it be observed that the word *ecclesia* ("church") signifies "assembly." Thus the Holy Church signifies the assembly of the faithful, and the individual Christian is a member of the Church of which it is said: "Draw near to me, ye unlearned, and gather yourselves together into the house of discipline."[243]

This Holy Church has four conditions: she is one, holy, catholic (i.e., universal), and strong (i.e., firmly established).

A. The Church is one

It must be noted that although various heretics have formed themselves into various sects, they do not belong to the Church, since they are so many divisions, whereas the Church is one: "One is my dove: my perfect one is but one."[244]

The unity of the Church arises from three sources:

[243] Ecclus. 51:31 (RSV = Sir. 51:23).
[244] Cant. 6:8 (RSV = Song of Sol. 6:8).

1. From the unity of faith, since all Christians who belong to the body of the Church have the same belief: "I beseech you . . . that you all speak the same thing and that there be no schisms among you."[245] "One Lord, one Faith, one Baptism."[246]

2. From the unity of hope, since all are confirmed in the hope of obtaining eternal life. Thus the Apostle says: "One body and one Spirit: as you are called in one hope of your calling.[247]

3. From the unity of charity, since all are united in loving God, and bound to one another in mutual love: "The glory which Thou hast given me, I have given to them — that they may be one as we also are one."[248]

If this love is true, it is evinced in the mutual solicitude and sympathy of the members: "That we may in all things grow up in Him who is the head, even Christ, from whom the whole body being compacted and fitly joined together, by what every joint supplieth, according to the operation in the measure of every part, maketh increase of the body, unto the edifying of itself in charity."[249] For each one ought to be of service to his neighbor by making use of the grace which God has bestowed on him.

Thus no man should think it of small account or allow himself to be cut off and expelled from this Church, for there is but one Church in which men find salvation, just as outside the Ark of Noah it was not possible for anyone to be saved.

---

[245] 1 Cor. 1:10.
[246] Eph. 4:5.
[247] Eph. 4:4.
[248] John 17:22.
[249] Eph. 4:15, 16.

B. The Church is holy

1. The Church as an assembly of the good. Let it be observed that there is also another assembly, that of the wicked: "I have hated the assembly of the malignant."[250] But this is an evil assembly, whereas Christ's Church is holy: "The temple of God is holy, which ye are."[251] Hence the words, *the Holy Church.*

2. The Church sanctifies its members. In this Church, the faithful are sanctified by four things:

a. By washing them. The faithful are washed with the blood of Christ, just as when a church is consecrated, it is cleansed materially: "He hath loved us and washed us from our sins in His own blood."[252] "Jesus, that He might sanctify the people by His own blood, suffered outside the gate."[253]

b. By anointing them. Just as a church is anointed, so also are the faithful anointed with a spiritual unction for sanctification. Otherwise they would not be Christians, since Christ is the same as Anointed. This unction is the grace of the Holy Spirit: "God who hath anointed us."[254] "Ye are sanctified . . . in the name of our Lord Jesus Christ."[255]

c. By the indwelling Trinity. They are sanctified by the indwelling Trinity, since wherever God dwells, that place is

[250] Ps. 25:5 (RSV = Ps. 26:5).
[251] 1 Cor. 3:17.
[252] Apoc. 1:5 (RSV = Rev. 1:5).
[253] Heb. 13:12.
[254] Cf. 2 Cor. 1:21.
[255] 1 Cor. 6:11.

holy: "Verily, this place is holy."[256] "Holiness becometh Thy house, O Lord."[257]

d. By invoking God over them. They are sanctified because God is invoked over them: "But Thou, O Lord, art among us, and Thy name hath been called upon us."[258]

Therefore, we must beware, seeing that we are thus sanctified, lest by sin we defile our soul which is God's temple: "If any man violate the temple of God, him shall God destroy."[259]

C. The Church is catholic ("universal")
We must observe that the Church is catholic ("universal"):

1. With regard to place, in that it is spread throughout the whole world, contrary to the teaching of the Donatists: "Your faith is spoken of in the whole world."[260] "Go ye into the whole world and preach the gospel to every creature."[261] Formerly, God was known only in Judea, whereas now He is known throughout the whole world. In this sense the Church has three parts: one is on earth, another in Heaven, the third in Purgatory.

2. With regard to the different conditions of humanity, inasmuch as no exceptions are made, for it includes master and servant, male and female: "There is neither male nor female."[262]

---

[256] Josh. 5:16.
[257] Ps. 92:5 (RSV = Ps. 93:5).
[258] Jer. 14:9.
[259] 1 Cor. 3:16, 17.
[260] Rom. 1:8.
[261] Mark 16:15.
[262] Gal. 3:28.

3. **With regard to time.** There have been those who said that the Church was to last until a certain time, but this is false, since this Church began from the time of Abel and will endure to the end of the world: "Behold, I am with you all days, even to the consummation of the world,"[263] and after the end of the world it will continue in Heaven.

D. The Church is firmly established
A house is said to be firmly established when:

1. **It has good foundations.** Now, the Church's chief foundation is Christ: "Other foundation no man can lay but that which is laid, which is Christ Jesus."[264] The Apostles and their doctrine are the Church's secondary foundation, from which she derives her stability. This is described where it is said that the city had "twelve foundations, wherein were [inscribed] the names of the twelve Apostles."[265] Hence the Church is called *apostolic*. Moreover, it was to indicate the stability of the Church that St. Peter is called the *head*.

2. **It remains standing.** A house also is proved to be firmly built if, however much it is shaken, it remains standing. And the Church has ever proved indestructible. Her persecutors have failed to destroy her. In fact, it was during times of persecution that the Church grew more and more and the persecutors themselves — and those whom the Church would destroy — came to nothing: "Whosoever shall fall on this stone shall be broken; but on whomsoever it shall fall, it shall grind him to powder."[266]

---

[263] Matt. 28:20.
[264] 1 Cor. 3:11.
[265] Apoc. 21:14 (RSV = Rev. 21:14).
[266] Matt. 21:44.

a. Errors have assailed her. In fact, the greater the number of errors that have arisen, the more has the truth been made manifest: "Men corrupt in mind, reprobate in faith: but they shall proceed no further."[267]

b. Demons have attacked her. Nor has the Church failed before the assaults of demons, for she is like a tower of refuge to all who fight against the Devil: "The name of the Lord is a strong tower."[268] Hence the Devil does his utmost to destroy the Church, but he does not prevail, for our Lord said that "the gates of Hell shall not prevail against it,"[269] as though to say, "They will war against thee, but they shall not overcome thee."

The result is that only the Church of Peter (to whom it was given to evangelize Italy when the disciples were sent to preach) was always strong in faith, whereas outside that Church there is either no faith at all or it is mingled with many errors. Yet the Church of Peter flourishes in faith and is immune from error. Nor need we wonder at this, since the Lord said to Peter, "I have prayed for thee, Peter, that thy faith may not fail."[270]

[267] 2 Tim. 3:8, 9.
[268] Prov. 18:10.
[269] Matt. 16:18.
[270] Luke 22:32.

XI

THE COMMUNION OF SAINTS,
THE FORGIVENESS OF SINS

A. Christ's good is communicated to all members

Just as in a physical body the operation of one member is conducive to the good of the whole body, so is it in a spiritual body such as the Church. And since all the faithful are one body, the good of one member is communicated to another: "Every one" — as the Apostle says — "members, one of another."[271] Therefore, among the points of Faith handed down by the Apostles is that there is a community of goods in the Church, and this is expressed in the words, *communion of saints*.

Now, of all the members of the Church, Christ is the principal, for He is the head: "He . . . hath made Him head over all the Church which is His body."[272] Accordingly, Christ's good is communicated to all Christians, even as the power in the head is shared by all the members.

B. The Sacraments communicate Christ's good

This communication is brought about through the Sacraments of the Church, in which the power of Christ's Passion operates, and whose effect is the bestowal of grace for the remission of sins.

[271] Rom. 12:5.
[272] Eph. 1:22, 23.

The Sacraments of the Church are seven in number:[273]

1. Baptism is the first, a spiritual regeneration. Just as a man cannot live in the flesh unless he is born in the flesh, so he cannot have the spiritual life of grace unless he is born again spiritually. This regeneration is effected by Baptism: "Unless a man be born again of water and the Holy Spirit, he cannot enter into the kingdom of God."[274] And it should be remarked that just as a man can be born only once, so is he baptized only once. For this reason the holy Fathers added[275] the words, *We acknowledge one Baptism.*

The power of Baptism consists in cleansing a man from all his sins as regards both guilt and punishment, for which reason no penance is imposed on those who receive Baptism, no matter how great their sins may have been. And if they were to die immediately after Baptism, they would rise at once to eternal life. Another result is that although no one but a priest may baptize *ex officio*, in cases of necessity anyone may baptize, provided he observes the form of Baptism, which is, "I baptize you in the name of the Father and of the Son and of the Holy Spirit."

This sacrament derives its efficacy from Christ's Passion: "All we who are baptized in Christ Jesus, are baptized in His death."[276] For this reason, just as Christ was three days in the tomb, so Baptism is conferred by a triple immersion.[277]

---

[273] The Seven Sacraments are discussed in greater detail in Part 4 of this book.

[274] John 3:5.

[275] To the Nicene Creed.

[276] Rom. 6:3.

[277] Baptism by immersion was still in vogue at the time of St. Thomas. Triple immersion was later replaced by the present rite, in which water is poured three times.

2. Confirmation. Just as those who are born in the body need to be fortified for the body to become operative, so those who are reborn in the spirit need to be fortified by the Holy Spirit. Hence the Apostles, in order to become strong, received the Holy Spirit after Christ's Ascension: "Stay you in the city till you be endued with power from on high."[278]

This power is conferred in the sacrament of Confirmation. Therefore, those who have charge of children ought to be most careful to see that they are confirmed, because great grace is bestowed in Confirmation. Besides, when he dies, one who is confirmed receives greater glory than one who has not been confirmed, because he has received more grace.

3. The Eucharist. In the life of the body, after a man is born and becomes strong, he requires food so that his life may be preserved and sustained; so also in the life of the spirit, after being fortified, he requires spiritual food, which is Christ's body: "Unless you shall eat of the flesh of the Son of man, and drink of His blood, you shall not have life in you."[279] For this reason the Church has ordained that every Christian once a year must receive the body of Christ, but worthily and with a clear conscience. For "he that eateth and drinketh unworthily" (i.e., being conscious of mortal sin which he has not confessed or from which he does not intend to abstain), "eateth and drinketh judgment to himself."[280]

4. Penance.[281] In the life of the body a man is sometimes sick, and unless he takes medicine, he will die. Likewise in the life of

[278] Luke 24:49.
[279] John 6:54 (RSV = John 6:53).
[280] 1 Cor. 11:29.
[281] Or *Confession*, now called *Reconciliation*.

the spirit, a man is sick on account of sin; thus, he needs medicine that he may be restored to health. This grace is bestowed in the sacrament of Penance: "who forgiveth all thy iniquities, who healeth all thy diseases."[282]

Three conditions are necessary for Penance: contrition (which is sorrow for sin together with a purpose of amendment); confession of sins without any omission; and satisfaction by means of good works.

5. The Anointing of the Sick.[283] In this life man encounters many obstacles which prevent him from being perfectly cleansed from his sins. And since no one can enter eternal life unless he is entirely cleansed from sin, another sacrament was needed whereby a man is cleansed from sin, delivered from his weakness, and prepared to enter the heavenly kingdom. This is the sacrament of the Anointing of the Sick.

That this sacrament does not always restore health to the body is because it may be that a man's life is not expedient for the salvation of his soul: "Is any man sick among you? Let him bring in the priests of the Church, and let them pray over him, anointing him in the name of the Lord; and the prayer of faith shall save the sick man and the Lord shall raise him up; and if he be in sins they shall be forgiven him."[284]

Accordingly it is clear how by the five foregoing sacraments a man obtains perfection in the spiritual life.

6. Holy Orders. Since, however, these same Sacraments need to be conferred by certain definite ministers, there arose the necessity of the sacrament of Orders, by means of which the above

[282] Ps. 102:3 (RSV = Ps. 103:3).
[283] Or *Last Rites* or *Extreme Unction*.
[284] James 5:14, 15.

86

Sacraments are dispensed. Nor need we consider the ministers' manner of life, if at times they fall into evil ways. The point to consider is the power of Christ, which gives efficacy to the Sacraments of which they are the dispensers: "Let a man so account of us as of the ministers of Christ, and the dispensers of the mysteries of God."[285] This, then, is the sixth sacrament, namely, Holy Orders.

7. **Matrimony,** in which if men lead a pure life, they are saved, since thereby they are enabled to live without mortal sin. Sometimes married people fall into venial sins, when their concupiscence does not lead them to act against the blessings of matrimony, but if they go beyond this they fall into mortal sin.

C. The forgiveness of sins

By these Seven Sacraments, we receive the remission of sins; so there follows immediately [in the Creed] *the forgiveness of sins,* which expresses our belief that the Apostles received the power to forgive sins. Thus, we must believe that the ministers of the Church (who derive this power from the Apostles, who received it from Christ) have power in the Church to bind and to loose; and that there is in the Church full power to forgive sins, which power, however, is possessed in various degrees descending from the Pope to other prelates.

It must also be observed that not only is the efficacy of Christ's Passion communicated to us, but also the merits of His life. And besides this, all the good deeds of holy men are communicated to those who are in a state of grace, because all are one: "I am a partaker with all them that fear Thee."[286]

So it is that a man who lives in the state of grace is a partaker of all the good that is done in the whole world; but in a special way

---

[285] 1 Cor. 4:1.
[286] Ps. 118:63 (RSV = Ps. 119:63).

those benefit for whom a good deed is done specifically. For one man can satisfy for another, as seen in those benefits to which many societies admit certain persons.

D. Benefits of the communion of saints

Through this communion, then, we derive a twofold benefit. One is that Christ's merit is communicated to all; the other is that one man's good is communicated to another. Thus, by the very fact that they are outside the Church, those who are excommunicated forfeit a share in all the good that is done, which is a greater loss than the loss of any temporal good. They also incur another risk, for it is clear that by this mutual assistance the Devil is hindered in his temptations; but that when a man is deprived of these aids, the Devil overcomes him with ease. For this reason in the early Church, when a person was excommunicated, it was not uncommon for him to experience in his body the assaults of the Devil.

XII

THE RESURRECTION OF THE BODY

Not only does the Holy Spirit sanctify the Church as regards our souls, but also it is by His power that our bodies will rise again: "Who raised up Jesus Christ our Lord from the dead."[287] "For by a man came death, and by a man came the resurrection of the dead."[288] So we believe, according to our Faith, that there will be a resurrection of the dead.

Here four points arise for our consideration: 1) the benefits we are to derive from our faith in the resurrection; 2) the condition of those who will rise again, as regards all in general; 3) their condition as regards those who are good; and 4) their condition as regards those who are wicked.

A. Faith in the resurrection benefits us

It is well to observe that faith and hope in the resurrection are profitable to us in four ways:

1. By removing the sadness occasioned by the death of others. It is impossible for a man not to grieve at the death of one who is dear to him, but inasmuch as he hopes that his dear one will rise again, his sorrow for his death is much alleviated: "We will

---

[287] Rom. 4:24.
[288] 1 Cor. 15:21.

89

not have you ignorant, brethren, concerning them that are asleep, that you be not sorrowful, even as others who have no hope."[289]

2. By removing the fear of death. For if man had no hope of another, better life after death, without doubt death would be very dreadful, and man would commit any wicked deed rather than taste death. But since we believe that there is another, better life to which we shall come after death, it is evident that no one should fear death or do anything wrong through fear of death: "That through death He might destroy him who had the empire of death (that is to say, the Devil) and might deliver them who through fear of death were all their lifetime subject to servitude."[290]

3. By making us anxious and diligent to perform good works. If man could look forward to no other life beyond this present life, he would have no great motive to do good works, because whatever he did would count for little, since his desire is not confined to any particular good at any particular time but looks to eternity. But because we believe that in return for what we do now we shall receive eternal reward at the resurrection, we apply ourselves to doing good: "If only in this life we have hope in Christ, we are of all men most miserable."[291]

4. By drawing us away from evil. Just as the hope of reward is a motive for good works, so fear of punishment (which we believe to be reserved for the wicked) is a motive for avoiding evil deeds: "And they that have done good things shall come forth

[289] 1 Thess. 4:12.
[290] Heb. 2:14, 15.
[291] 1 Cor. 15:19.

unto the resurrection of life; but they that have done evil, unto the resurrection of judgment."[292]

B. The characteristics of all risen bodies
Four conditions characterize all who will rise again:

1. The identity of the risen body. The same body that is now with its flesh and bones will rise again. Some have maintained that this very body which is corruptible here below will not rise again, but this is contrary to the Apostle's statement that "this corruptible must put on incorruption."[293] And Sacred Scripture says that by God's power the same body will come back to life: "I shall be clothed again in my skin; and in my flesh I shall see God."[294]

2. The quality of risen bodies. They will be of a different quality from that which they have now. Thus both good and wicked will rise with incorruptible bodies, since the good will be forever in glory and the wicked in everlasting punishment: "This corruptible must put on incorruption and this mortal put on immortality."[295] And since the body will be incorruptible and immortal there will be no use for food or sexual relations: "In the resurrection they will neither marry nor be given in marriage, but will be as the angels in Heaven."[296] This is against the Jews and Mohammedans: "Nor shall he return any more into his house."[297]

---

[292] John 5:29.
[293] 1 Cor. 15:53.
[294] Job 19:26.
[295] 1 Cor. 15:53.
[296] Matt. 22:30.
[297] Job 7:10.

3. The integrity of risen bodies. All (both good and evil) will rise with all the bodily integrity that pertains to the perfection of man. Therefore, no one will be blind or lame or suffering from any defect: "The dead shall rise again incorruptible,"[298] immune to the corruptions of the present life.

4. The age of risen bodies. All will rise again at the perfect age, namely, thirty-two or thirty-three years. The reason is that those who have not reached that age are not at the perfect age, and the old have already passed it. So young people and children will receive what they lack, and the old will be restored to what they have lost: "Until we all meet in the unity of faith . . . unto a perfect man, unto the measure of the age of the fullness of Christ."[299]

C. Qualities of the glorified bodies of the blessed[300]
The good will have a special glory, because the saints will have glorified bodies, which will be endowed with four gifts:

1. Impassibility.[301] "It is sown in dishonor; it shall rise in glory."[302] "God shall wipe away all tears from their eyes; and death shall be no more. Neither mourning, nor crying, nor sorrow shall be any more; for the former things are passed away."[303]

2. Brilliancy. "The just shall shine as the sun in their Father's kingdom."[304]

[298] 1 Cor. 15:52.
[299] Eph. 4:13.
[300] See also "The Gifts of the Sacraments" in Part 4.
[301] The state of being beyond the reach of suffering or harm.
[302] 1 Cor. 15:43.
[303] Rev. 21:4.
[304] Matt. 13:43.

3. Agility. "The just shall shine and shall run to and fro like sparks among the reeds.[305]

4. Subtlety. "It is sown a natural body: it shall rise a spiritual body."[306] Not that it will be a spirit altogether, but it will be wholly subject to the spirit.

D. Qualities of the bodies of the damned

It must be observed that the state of the damned will be contrary to that of the blessed, since they will be in a state of eternal punishment, to which a fourfold evil condition attaches:

1. Passibility. Their bodies will be passible and yet never destroyed, for they will burn forever in the fire but will never be consumed: "Their worm shall not die, and their fire shall not be quenched."[307]

2. Darkness. Their bodies will be dark: "Their countenances shall be as faces burnt."[308]

3. Heaviness. Their bodies will be weighed down, for the soul will be as it were chained in their bodies: "To bind their kings with fetters and their nobles with manacles of iron."[309]

4. Carnality. Both body and soul will be carnal, so to speak: "The beasts have rotted in their dung."[310]

[305] Wisd. 3:7.
[306] 1 Cor. 15:44.
[307] Isa. 66:24.
[308] Isa. 13:8.
[309] Ps. 149:8.
[310] Joel 1:17.

XIII

AND LIFE EVERLASTING.
AMEN

It is fitting that the last article of Faith in the Creed should give expression to that which is the end of all our desires (namely, eternal life) in the words, *And life everlasting. Amen.* This article is contradicted by those who hold that the soul perishes with the body. If this were true, man would be in the same condition as the beasts. To those who hold this opinion we may apply the words of the Psalmist: "Man, whereas he was in honor, understood it not; he hath been compared to senseless beasts, and made like to them."[311]

For the human soul is likened to God in respect to immortality, whereas it is like the beasts in respect to sensuality. So when a man believes that his soul dies with his body, he abandons his likeness to God and becomes like a beast. Against these it is said: "They . . . hoped not for the wages of righteousness, nor esteemed the honor of holy souls. For God created man incorruptible, and to the image of His own likeness He made him."[312]

A. The nature of the eternal life of the blessed

In this article we must first consider what *eternal life* is. The first thing to be noted is that in eternal life, man is united to God. God

[311] Ps. 48:21 (RSV = Ps. 49:12).
[312] Wisd. 2:22, 23.

Himself is our reward and the end of all our labors: "I am thy protector and thy reward exceeding great."[313]

Union with God consists in six things:

1. Perfect vision of God. Union with God consists in seeing God perfectly: "We see now through a glass darkly, but then face-to-face."[314]

2. Perfect knowledge of God. Union with God consists in knowing God perfectly. For the better one is known, the more perfectly one is loved: "The Lord hath said it, whose fire is in Sion, and His furnace in Jerusalem."[315]

3. Perfect praise of God. Union with God consists in praising God perfectly: "We shall behold, we shall love, and we shall praise," as St. Augustine says.[316] "Joy and gladness shall be found therein, thanksgiving and the voice of praise."[317]

4. Perfect fulfillment of desires. Eternal life is the perfect fulfillment of desires, since each of the blessed will have more than he desired or hoped for. The reason is that in this life no man can fulfill his desires, nor can any creature satisfy a man's craving, for God alone satisfies and infinitely surpasses man's desire, which for that reason is never at rest except in God: "Thou hast made us for thyself, O Lord, and our heart is restless until it rests in Thee."[318] And since in Heaven the saints will possess God

---

[313] Gen. 15:1.
[314] 1 Cor. 13:12.
[315] Isa. 31:9. This point is found in the Vives edition, ch. 15.
[316] *The City of God*, Bk. 22, ch. 30.
[317] Isa. 51:3.
[318] St. Augustine, *Confessions*, Bk. 1, ch. 1.

perfectly, it is evident that their desires will be satisfied and that their glory will surpass their expectations. Hence our Lord said, "Enter into the joy of thy Lord,"[319] which St. Augustine explains by saying, "Their whole joy will not enter into the joyful, but the joyful will enter into joy." "I shall be satisfied when Thy glory shall appear."[320] And again: "Who filleth thy desire with good things,"[321] because whatever is delightful will be there superabundantly:

a. Pleasure. Thus, if we desire pleasure, there will be supreme and most perfect delight, in that its object will be God, the sovereign good: "Then shalt thou abound in delights in the Almighty."[322] "At Thy right hand are delights even to the end."[323]

b. Honors. Likewise, if we desire honors, all honor will be there. The highest ambition of a man, if he is a layman, is to be a king; and if he is a cleric, to be a bishop. Both these honors are there: "Thou hast made us to our God a kingdom and priests."[324] "Behold how they are numbered among the children of God."[325]

c. Knowledge. Again, if we desire knowledge, there will be most perfect knowledge, because we shall know all the natures of things and all truth — and whatever we wish, we

[319] Matt. 25:21.
[320] Ps. 16:15 (RSV = Ps. 17:15).
[321] Ps. 102:5 (RSV = Ps. 103:5).
[322] Job 22:26.
[323] Ps. 15:11 (RSV = Ps. 16:11).
[324] Apoc. 5:10 (RSV = Rev. 5:10).
[325] Wisd. 5:5.

shall know. We shall possess whatever we desire to possess, together with eternal life itself: "All good things came to me together with her."[326] "To the righteous their desire shall be given."[327]

5. Perfect security. Eternal life consists in perfect security. In this world there is no perfect security, since the more someone has and the higher his position, the more he has to fear and the more he wants. But in eternal life there is neither sorrow, nor toil, nor fear: "He shall enjoy abundance without fear of evils."[328]

6. Companionship of the blessed. Eternal life consists in the pleasant companionship of all the blessed, a companionship that is replete with delight, since each one will possess all good things together with the blessed. They will all love one another as themselves, and therefore will rejoice in the happiness of others' goods as their own. Consequently, the joy and gladness of one will be as great as the joy of all: "The dwelling in thee is as it were of all rejoicing."[329]

B. The nature of the eternal death of the wicked
The saints in Heaven will have all these things and many more that surpass description. The wicked, on the other hand, in everlasting death will have no less sorrow and pain than the good have joy and glory.

1. Separation from God and from all good things will aggravate the punishment of the wicked. This is the pain of loss, which

[326] Wisd. 7:11.
[327] Prov. 10:24.
[328] Prov. 1:33.
[329] Ps. 86:7 (RSV = Ps. 87:7).

corresponds to aversion and surpasses the pain of sense: "Cast out the unprofitable servant into outer darkness."[330] In this life the wicked have internal darkness, namely, the darkness of sin, but then they will have outer darkness besides.

2. Remorse of conscience will aggravate their punishment: "I will reprove thee and set before thy face."[331] "Groaning for anguish of spirit."[332] Nevertheless their regret and anguish will be useless, for it will not be on account of the hatred of evil, but on account of grief for their punishment.

3. Intensity of the pains of sense (inflicted by the fires of Hell, which will torture both soul and body) will aggravate their punishment. This is a most painful punishment, according to the saints: for they will be as though always dying but never dead and never going to die. For this reason it is described as everlasting death, seeing that just as a dying man is in extreme pain, even so are those who are in Hell: "They are laid in Hell like sheep; death shall feed upon them."[333]

4. Despair of salvation will aggravate their punishment, for if it were given them to hope for deliverance from their torture, their punishment would be alleviated. But since they have lost all hope, their pains are exceedingly aggravated: "Their worm shall not die, and their fire shall not be quenched."[334] Thus we can realize the difference between doing good and doing evil, since good works lead to life while wicked deeds drag us to

[330] Matt. 25:30.
[331] Ps. 49:21 (RSV = Ps. 50:21).
[332] Wisd. 5:3.
[333] Ps. 48:15 (RSV = Ps. 49:14).
[334] Isa. 66:24.

death. For this reason man should frequently call these things to mind, since thereby he is urged to good things and drawn away from evil.

Thus, significantly, the Creed ends with the words, *life everlasting*, that it may ever remain more and more impressed on the memory.

To this life everlasting may we be brought
by our Lord Jesus Christ, who is God,
blessed for ever and ever! Amen.

Part 2

How Christians Should Pray

The Lord's Prayer
The Hail Mary

THE LORD'S PRAYER

Our Father, who art in Heaven,
hallowed be Thy name.
Thy kingdom come.
Thy will be done on earth as it is in Heaven.
Give us this day our daily bread
and forgive us our trespasses
as we forgive those who trespass against us.
And lead us not into temptation
but deliver us from evil. Amen.

THE HAIL MARY

Hail Mary, full of grace,
the Lord is with thee.
Blessed art thou among women,
and blessed is the fruit of thy womb.[335]

---

[335] At the time of St. Thomas, the Hail Mary consisted only of
what is now the first part, ending with the words, *the fruit of
thy womb*. The addition of the Holy Name of Jesus probably
began about the time of St. Thomas. The second half —
*Holy Mary, Mother of God, pray for us sinners now and at the
hour of our death* — was added during the sixteenth cen-
tury. Cf. *Catholic Encyclopedia*, s.v. *Hail Mary*.

I

THE LORD'S PRAYER

Among all prayers the Lord's Prayer[336] stands preeminent, for it excels in the five conditions required in prayer: confidence, rectitude, order, devotion, and humility.

A. Conditions required for prayer.

1. **Confidence.** Prayer should be confident: "Let us go with confidence to the throne of grace"[337] (and with fullness of faith: "Let him ask in faith, nothing wavering"[338]). There can be no doubt that the Lord's Prayer affords the greatest security, since it was framed by our Advocate and most wise Petitioner, in whom are "all the treasures of wisdom"[339] and of whom it is said: "We have an advocate with the Father, Jesus Christ, the just."[340] Hence Cyprian says: "Seeing that we have Christ as an advocate with the Father for our sins, we should employ the words of our advocate when we seek forgiveness of our sins."[341]

---

[336] Cf. *Summa Theologica*, II-II, Q. 83, art. 9.
[337] Heb. 4:16.
[338] James 1:6.
[339] Col. 2:3.
[340] 1 John 2:1.
[341] *De Orat. Dom.*

The trustworthiness of this prayer is even more apparent because He who (with the Father) hears our prayer, Himself taught us how to pray, according to Psalm 90:15: "He shall cry to me, and I will hear him." For that reason Cyprian says that "to plead with our Lord in His own words betokens the prayer of an intimate and devoted friend."[342] Consequently, this prayer is never fruitless, seeing that according to St. Augustine venial sins are forgiven by means of it.[343]

2. Rectitude. Prayer should have rectitude, so that we ask God for that which is good for us. For Damascene says that "to pray is to ask fitting things of God."[344] It often happens that our prayers are not granted because we ask for that which is not good for us: "You ask and receive not, because you ask amiss."[345]

Now, it is no easy matter to know what we should pray for, since it is difficult to know what we ought to desire. For if it is right to pray for a certain thing, it must be right to desire it. For this reason the Apostle says that "we know not what we should pray for as we ought."[346] Now, Christ is our teacher; it belongs to Him to teach us what we ought to pray for. Thus His disciples said to Him, "Lord, teach us to pray."[347] It follows, then, that we pray most rightly when we ask for what He taught us to pray for. Hence St. Augustine says, "If we would pray rightly and fittingly, we should say nothing else but what is contained in this prayer of our Lord."[348]

[342] Ibid.

[343] *Enchiridion* 78; cf. St. Thomas Aquinas, *Summa Theologica*, I-II, Q. 74, art. 8, ad 6.

[344] St. John Damascene, *De Fide Orth.*, 3, ch. 24.

[345] James 4:3.

[346] Rom. 8:26.

[347] Luke 11:1.

[348] *Ep. 130, ad Probam.*

3. Order. As desire should be orderly, so should prayer, since it is the expression of desire. Now, the right order is that our desires and prayers should prefer spiritual goods to carnal goods and heavenly things to earthly things: "Seek ye first the kingdom of God and His justice, and all these things shall be added unto you."[349] Our Lord teaches us to observe this order in the Lord's Prayer, in which we pray first for heavenly and afterward for earthly blessings.

4. Devoutness. Prayer should be devout, because the unction of devotion makes the sacrifice of prayer acceptable to God: "In Thy name I will lift up my hands; let my soul be filled as with marrow and fatness."[350] Yet it often happens that devotion grows cool through prayer being too long. For that reason our Lord warned us against praying at unnecessary length: "When you are praying, speak not much."[351] And St. Augustine says to Proba: "Beware of praying with many words: it is fervent attention that secures a hearing."[352] Hence the brevity of the Lord's Prayer.

Now, devotion arises from charity, which is the love of God and of our neighbor, and both of these are indicated in the Lord's Prayer. In order to express our love of God we call Him *Father*, and in order to indicate love of our neighbor we pray for all in general: *Our Father . . . forgive us our trespasses* (since it is through love of our neighbor that we make this petition).

5. Humility. Prayer should be humble: "He hath had regard to the prayer of the humble."[353] This is seen in the story of the

---

[349] Matt. 6:33.
[350] Ps. 62:5-6 (RSV = Ps. 63:4-5).
[351] Matt. 6:7.
[352] *Ep. 130, ad Probam.*
[353] Ps. 101:18 (RSV = Ps. 102:17).

Pharisee and the publican,[354] and is expressed in the words of Judith: "The prayer of the humble and the meek hath always pleased Thee."[355] This same humility is observed in the Lord's Prayer since true humility consists in not presuming on our own strength, but in trusting to obtain all things from the power of God.

B. Benefits of prayer

Prayer brings about three benefits:

1. It remedies evils. Prayer is an efficacious and useful remedy against all kinds of evils. Hence it delivers a man from sins already committed: "Thou hast forgiven the wickedness of my sin; for this shall every godly man pray to Thee."[356] Thus the thief on his cross prayed and obtained pardon: "This day shalt thou be with me in Paradise."[357] So also the publican prayed and "went down to his house justified."[358]

Prayer also frees man from the fear of future sin and from trials and despondency: "Is any one of you in trouble? Let him pray."[359] Again, it delivers him from persecutors and enemies: "Instead of making me a return for my love, they decried me; but I gave myself to prayer."[360]

2. It obtains that which we desire. Prayer is efficacious and useful for obtaining whatever we desire: "All things whatsoever

[354] Luke 18:10-14.
[355] Jth. 9:16.
[356] Ps. 31:5, 6 (RSV = Ps. 32:5, 6).
[357] Luke 23:43.
[358] Luke 18:14.
[359] Cf. James 5:13.
[360] Ps. 108:4 (RSV = Ps. 109:4).

ye ask, when ye pray, believe that you shall receive."[361] And if our prayer is not granted, it is either because it lacks constancy, in that "we should pray always and never faint,"[362] or because we ask for what is less conducive to our salvation. Thus St. Augustine says, "Of His bounty, the Lord often grants not what we seek, so as to bestow something preferable." We have an example of this in Paul who three times prayed for the removal of the thorn in his flesh, and yet was not heard.[363]

3. It establishes friendship with God. Prayer is profitable because it makes us the familiars of God: "Let my prayer be directed as incense in Thy sight."[364]

[361] Mark 11:24.
[361] Luke 18:1.
[362] 2 Cor. 12:7-9.
[364] Ps. 140:2 (RSV = Ps. 141:2).

II

OUR FATHER

Accordingly our Lord begins, *Our Father*. We must consider two things here: 1) in what sense God is our Father, and 2) what we owe Him because He is our Father.

A. Why we call God *Father*

1. He created us. We call God *Father* because He created us in a special way — namely, in His own image and likeness which He did not impress on other creatures here below: "He is thy Father who made thee, and created thee."[365]

2. He governs us. We also call God *Father* because He governs us. For although He governs *all* things, yet He governs us as masters of ourselves whereas He governs other things as slaves of His will: "Thy Providence, O Father, governs all things."[366] "Thou disposest of us with great favor."[367]

3. He adopted us. We call God *Father* because He has adopted us. For He endowed other creatures with trifling gifts, but to us

---

[365] Deut. 32:6.
[366] Wisd. 14:3.
[367] Wisd. 12:18.

He granted the inheritance, because (as the Apostle says) we are His sons "and if sons, heirs also. You have not received the spirit of bondage again in fear, but you have received the spirit of adoption of sons whereby we cry, *Abba* ('Father')."[368]

B. What we owe God as our Father
Our debt to God is fourfold:

1. Honor. We owe God honor: "If I am Father, where is my honor?"[369] This honor consists in three things:

a. In reference to Him, we should honor God by giving Him praise: "The sacrifice of praise shall honor me."[370] Moreover, this praise should be not only on our lips, but also in our heart: "This people honoreth me with their lips, but their heart is far from me."[371]

b. In reference to ourselves, we should honor God by purity of body: "Glorify and bear God in your body."[372]

c. In reference to our neighbor, we should honor God by judging him justly: "The king's honor loveth judgment."[373]

2. Imitation. We owe God imitation, for He is our Father: "Thou shalt call me Father and shalt not cease to walk after me."[374]

---

[368] Rom. 8:17, 15.
[369] Mal. 1:6.
[370] Ps. 49:23 (RSV = Ps. 50:23).
[371] Isa. 29:13.
[372] 1 Cor. 6:20.
[373] Ps. 98:4 (RSV = Ps. 99:4).
[374] Jer. 3:19.

This is done in three ways:

a. By loving Him. We imitate God by loving Him: "Be ye imitators of God as most dear children and walk in love."[375] And this must be in the heart.

b. By showing mercy. We imitate God by being merciful, because mercy is bound to accompany love: "Be ye merciful."[376] And this must be in deed.

c. By being perfect. We imitate God by being perfect, since love and mercy should be perfect: "Be ye perfect as also your heavenly Father is perfect."[377]

3. Obedience. We owe God obedience: "Shall we not much more obey the Father of spirits?"[378] We owe him obedience:

a. Because of His dominion, for He is the Lord: "All that the Lord hath said will we do, and be obedient."[379]

b. Because of His example, since His true Son was made obedient to the Father unto death.[380]

c. Because obedience is good for us: "I will play before the Lord who hath chosen me."[381]

---

[375] Eph. 5:1, 2.
[376] Luke 6:36.
[377] Matt. 5:48.
[378] Heb. 12:9.
[379] Exod. 24:7.
[380] Phil. 2:8.
[381] Cf. 2 Kings 6:21, 22 (RSV = 2 Sam. 6:21, 22).

4. Patience. We owe God patience under His chastening: "My son, reject not the correction of the Lord and do not faint when thou art chastised by Him: for whom the Lord loveth, He chastiseth even as a father the son in whom he delighteth."[382]

C. What we owe our neighbor (*our* Father)

From this we are given to understand that we owe our neighbor two things:

1. Love. We owe our neighbor love, because he is our brother, seeing that we are God's children: "He that loveth not his brother whom he seeth, how can he love God, whom he seeth not?"[383]

2. Reverence. We owe our neighbor reverence, because he is a child of God: "Have we not all one Father? Hath not one God created us? Why then doth every one of us despise his brother?"[384] "Outdo one another in showing honor."[385]

We do this for the sake of its fruits, since God Himself "became to all that obey Him the cause of eternal salvation."[386]

---

[382] Prov. 3:11, 12.
[383] 1 John 4:20.
[384] Mal. 2:10.
[385] Rom. 12:10.
[386] Heb. 5:9.

III

WHO ART IN HEAVEN

A. Confidence in prayer

Of all the things required of us when we pray, confidence is of great avail: "Let him ask in faith, nothing wavering."[387]

For this reason our Lord in teaching us how to pray mentions those things which instill confidence in us, such as the loving kindness of a father implied in the words, *Our Father*. Thus He says, "If ye being evil know how to give good gifts to your children, how much more shall your heavenly Father give the good Spirit to them that ask Him?"[388]

B. Meaning of *who art in Heaven*

Such also is the greatness of His power that He says, *Who art in Heaven*. Thus it is written: "Unto Thee have I lifted up mine eyes, who dwelleth in the heavens."[389]

The phrase *who art in Heaven* may be taken to refer to three things:

1. The glory of Heaven (which prepares him who prays).

Who art in Heaven prepares the man who prays: "Before prayer,

[387] James 1:6.
[388] Luke 11:13.
[389] Ps. 122:1 (RSV = Ps. 123:1).

113

prepare thy soul."[390] In this way, *in Heaven* signifies the glory of Heaven: "Your reward is very great in Heaven."[391]

We should prepare for prayer:

a. By imitating heavenly things, for a son should imitate his father: "As we have borne the image of the earthly, let us bear the image of the heavenly."[392]

b. By contemplating heavenly things, for a man is wont to turn his thoughts more often toward where his father is and where the things he loves are: "Wheresoever thy treasure is, there also is thy heart."[393] "Our conversation is in Heaven."[394]

c. By searching for heavenly things, so that from Him who is in Heaven we seek nothing but what is heavenly: "Seek the things that are above where Christ is."[395]

2. The nearness of the Hearer (in the saints). *Who art in Heaven* may be taken to indicate the handiness of the Hearer, insofar as God is near to us. Thus *in cælis* (literally, "in the heavens") would mean "in the saints" in whom God dwells: "Thou, O Lord, art among us."[396] For the saints are called *the heavens* according to the Psalm: "The heavens declare the glory of God."[397]

Now, God dwells in the saints in three ways:

---

[390] Ecclus. 18:23 (RSV = Sir. 18:23).
[391] 1 Cor. 15:49.
[392] Matt. 5:12.
[393] Matt. 6:21.
[394] Phil. 3:20.
[395] Col. 3:1.
[396] Jer. 14:9.
[397] Ps. 18:2 (RSV = Ps. 19:1).

a. By faith: "That Christ may dwell in your hearts by faith";[398]

b. By love: "He that dwelleth in love, dwelleth in God, and God in him";[399] and

c. By the fulfillment of His commandments: "If any man love me, he will keep my word, and my Father will love him, and we will come unto him, and make our abode with him."[400]

3. The power of the Hearer. *Who art in Heaven* may be taken as referring to the power of the Hearer, so that *the heavens* would signify the heavenly bodies. Not that God is confined within corporeal heavens (for "The heaven and heaven of heavens cannot contain Thee"[401]) but rather that:

a. God is all-seeing in His survey of things because He views them from on high: "He hath looked down from the height of His sanctuary";[402] and that,

b. He surpasses all things in His might: "The Lord hath prepared His throne in Heaven";[403] and that,

c. He dwells in an unchangeable eternity: "Thou endurest forever. . . . Thy years shall not fail."[404] Hence it is said of

---

[398] Eph. 3:17.
[399] 1 John 4:16.
[400] John 14:23.
[401] 3 Kings 8:27 (RSV = 1 Kings 8:27).
[402] Ps. 101:20 (RSV = Ps. 102:19).
[403] Ps. 102:19 (RSV = Ps. 103:19).
[404] Ps. 101:13, 28 (RSV = Ps. 102:12, 27).

Christ: "I will make His throne as the days of Heaven."[405]
Thus the Philosopher says that on account of the heavens
being incorruptible, all are agreed that Heaven is the abode
of spirits.[406]

C. These words give us confidence in prayer
Accordingly [as will be shown], the words, *Who art in Heaven* in-
spire us with confidence in praying, because of: 1) the power of
Him to whom we pray; 2) our familiar relations with Him; and 3)
the nature of our petitions.

1. Because of the power of Him to whom we pray, which is
implied if by *Heaven* we understand the corporeal heavens. Although God is not confined within corporeal space (since it is
said: "I fill Heaven and earth"[407]) yet He is said to be in the corporeal heavens in order to indicate two things: a) the extent of
His power, and b) the sublimity of His nature:

a. The extent of His power is maintained against those who
assert that all happenings are the necessary result of fate as de-
pendent on the heavenly bodies (according to which opinion
it would be useless to seek to obtain anything by praying to
God). But this is foolish because God is said to be in Heaven
in the sense that He is the Lord of the heavens and of the
stars: "The Lord hath prepared His throne in the heavens."

b. The sublimity of His nature is maintained against those
who in praying suppose and fancy God to exist under certain
corporeal images. Thus God is said to be *in Heaven* to indicate

[405] Ps. 88:30 (RSV = Ps. 89:29).
[406] Aristotle was known as "The Philosopher"; *De Caelo*, 1.
[407] Jer. 23:24.

His supereminence by means of that which is highest among sensible things. For He surpasses all things (including man's desire and understanding). Hence it is impossible to think or desire anything but what is less than God. Thus it is said: "Behold, God is great, exceeding our knowledge"[408] and "The Lord is high above all nations"[409] and "To whom have you likened God?"[410]

2. Because of our familiar relations with God, which are indicated if we take *the heavens* to signify the saints. For on account of His exalted nature, some have asserted that He did not care for human affairs, citing Job: "He walketh about the poles of Heaven, and He doth not consider our things."[411] Thus we need to bear in mind that He is near to us, nay, within us, since He is said to be in the heavens, i.e., in the saints who are called *the heavens*: "The heavens declare the glory of God" and "Thou, O Lord, art among us." Now, for two reasons this brings confidence to those who pray:

a. God's nearness. Confidence comes from God's nearness: "The Lord is nigh unto all that call upon Him."[412] Hence it is said: "But thou when thou prayest enter into thy chamber,"[413] i.e., into your heart.

b. The patronage of the saints. Confidence comes from our ability (by the patronage of the saints) to obtain what we ask

---

[408] Job 36:26.
[409] Ps. 112:4 (RSV = Ps. 113:4).
[410] Isa. 40:18.
[411] Job 22:14.
[412] Ps. 144:18 (RSV = Ps. 145:18).
[413] Matt. 6:6.

for: "Turn to some of the saints."[414] "Pray for one another that you may be saved."[415]

3. Because of the eternal goods for which we pray. The usefulness and fittingness of prayer are indicated by the words *in Heaven*, if by *Heaven* is understood spiritual and eternal goods in which beatitude consists, and this is for two reasons:

a. This awakens heavenly desire. Thereby, the words *in Heaven* increase our desire for heavenly things since our desire must tend toward where our Father dwells, because there is our inheritance: "Seek the things that are above." "Unto an inheritance incorruptible . . . reserved in Heaven for you."[416]

b. This gives heavenly life. Prayer gives life a spiritual form and conforms us to our heavenly Father: "Such as is the heavenly, such also are they that are heavenly."[417] These two (heavenly desire and heavenly life) equip a man for prayer and enable him to pray in a fitting manner.

[414] Job 5:1.
[415] James 5:16.
[416] 1 Pet. 1:4.
[417] 1 Cor. 15:48.

IV

HALLOWED BE THY NAME
(First Petition)

In this first petition we ask that God's name be manifested and heralded in us.

A. Characteristics of God's name

1. **God's name is wonderful,** since in all creatures it works wonders. Thus our Lord said, "In my name they shall cast out devils; they shall speak strange tongues; they shall take up serpents; and if they drink any deadly thing it shall not hurt them."[418]

2. **God's name is lovable:** "There is no other name under Heaven given among men whereby we must be saved,"[419] and we should all desire to be saved. We have an example in St. Ignatius, to whom Christ's name was so dear that when Trajan ordered him to deny it, he answered that it could not be dragged from his mouth. And when the emperor threatened to behead him so as to take Christ's name out of his mouth, he replied, "Even though you take it from my mouth you will never take it from my heart; for it is imprinted on my heart, and therefore I

---

[418] Mark 16:17, 18.
[419] Acts 4:12.

cannot cease to invoke it." Hearing this and wishing to put it to the test, Trajan, after the servant of God had been beheaded, commanded his heart to be taken out, where it was found to be inscribed with Christ's name in "letters of gold" for he had en-graved this name "as a seal on his heart."

3. God's name is venerable. Thus the Apostle says, "At the name of Jesus every knee should bow, of things in Heaven, on earth, and under the earth."[420] *Of things in Heaven* refers to the angels and the blessed; *of things on earth* refers to the inhabitants of the earth, who bow for love of the Heaven which they desire to obtain; and *of things under the earth* refers to the damned, who do so out of fear.

4. God's name is ineffable, because no tongue can describe it, for which reason sometimes it is explained with reference to cre-ated things. God's name is compared *to a rock* by reason of its stability: "On this rock I will build my church";[421] *to fire*, because of its power to cleanse, since just as fire cleanses denser metals, so does God purify the hearts of sinners: "Thy God is a consum-ing fire";[422] and *to light*, by reason of its enlightenment, for just as light banishes darkness, so the name of God banishes darkness from the mind: "My God, enlighten Thou my darkness."[423]

B. The meaning of *hallowed*
We pray then that this name be made manifest, that it may be known and hallowed. Now, the Latin word *sanctum* ("holy" or "hallowed") admits of a threefold meaning:

[420] Phil. 2:10.
[421] Matt. 16:18; "And the rock was Christ": 1 Cor. 10:4.
[422] Deut. 4:24.
[423] Ps. 17:29 (RSV = Ps. 18:28).

1. **"Firm"**: *Sanctum* ("hallowed") is the same as *sancitum* ("firm"). Therefore all the blessed in Heaven are called saints, because they are firmly established in eternal bliss; but no one is a saint on earth, where all are continually changeable: "I sank away from Thee, and I wandered too much astray from Thee, my support."[424]

2. **"The opposite of earthly" (i.e., "the opposite of sinners")**: *Sanctum* ("hallowed") may be rendered "unearthly." The saints in Heaven have no earthly affections. Thus the Apostle says, "I count all things but as dung, that I may gain Christ."[425]

Earth signifies "sinners":

a. **As regards production,** since if the earth is not cultivated, it brings forth thorns and thistles. In like manner, the sinner's soul, unless it is cultivated by grace, brings forth nothing but the thistles and pricks of sins: "Thorns and thistles shall it bring forth to thee."[426]

b. **As regards darkness,** since the earth is dark and opaque as the sinner is dark and opaque: "Darkness was on the face of the abyss."[427]

c. **As regards aridity,** because earth as a dry element will not cohere without moisture to bind it together. So God placed the earth above the waters,[428] because the moisture of the waters holds together the arid and dry earth. In the same

[424] St. Augustine, *Confessions*, Bk 2, ch. 10.
[425] Phil. 3:8.
[426] Gen. 3:18.
[427] Gen. 1:2.
[428] Ps. 135:6 (RSV = Ps. 136:6).

way, the sinner's soul is arid and devoid of humor: "My soul is as earth without water unto Thee."[429]

3. **"Washed in blood":** *Sanctum* ("hallowed") may be understood as "washed in blood" (*sanguine tinctum*), since the saints in Heaven are called saints because they have been washed in blood: "These are they who came out of great tribulation and have washed their robes . . . in the blood of the Lamb."[430] And, "He hath washed us from our sins in His blood."[431]

---

[429] Ps. 142:6 (RSV = Ps. 143:6).
[430] Apoc. 7:14 (RSV = Rev. 7:14).
[431] Apoc. 1:5 (RSV = Rev. 1:5).

V

THY KINGDOM COME
(Second Petition)

A. The gift of piety

As already stated, the Holy Spirit makes us love, desire, and pray rightly. He begins by causing in us fear by which we ask that God's name be hallowed. Another gift of the Holy Spirit is *piety*.

Now, piety, properly speaking, is a disposition of kindliness and devotion toward one's father, and toward all those who are in distress. Since God is our Father, as we have made evident, it follows that not only ought we to revere and fear Him, but we also ought to have a sweet and devout disposition toward Him. This makes us pray that His kingdom may come: "We should live righteously and piously in this present world, looking for the blessed hope and manifestation of the glory of the great God."[432]

B. Reasons for this petition

It may be asked, "Since the kingdom of God always was, why must we ask for it to come?" The answer may be understood in three ways:

1. So that all things may become subject to Him. Sometimes a king has only the *right* to a kingdom or throne, but as yet has not

---

[432] Titus 2:12.

been proclaimed king because the inhabitants are not as yet subjected to him. In this sense, his kingdom or throne will come when those men are subject to him.

Now, God by His very essence and nature is Lord of all. And Christ is Lord of all (not only as God but as man by reason of His Godhead): "He gave Him power and glory and a kingdom."[433] Consequently, all things ought to be subject to Him. However, they are not subject as yet, but will be at the end of the world: "He must reign until He hath put all His enemies under His feet."[434] Therefore, it is for this that we pray when we say, *Thy kingdom come*.

In making this petition, we have a threefold purpose: a) the safeguarding of the just; b) the punishment of the wicked; and c) the destruction of death.

a. The safeguarding of the just. Man is subject to Christ in two ways, either willingly or unwillingly. Since God's will is efficacious, it must be fulfilled outright; and since God wills all things to be subject to Christ, one of two things is necessary: either that men do the will of God by submitting to His commandments (as the just do) or else that God wreak His will on men by punishing them (as He will do on sinners and on His enemies at the end of the world): "Until I make thy enemies thy footstool."[435] For these reasons, the saints are enjoined to ask that God's kingdom may come (i.e., that they may be wholly subject to Him).

b. The punishment of the wicked. To sinners this is repellent, since their asking that God's kingdom may come is

[433] Dan. 7:14.
[434] 1 Cor. 15:25.
[435] Ps. 109:1 (RSV = Ps. 110:1).

nothing less than their praying that by God's will they may be condemned to punishment: "Woe to them that desire the day of the Lord."[436]

c. The destruction of death. The result [of the coming of the kingdom] will be the destruction of death. Since Christ is life, in His kingdom there can be no death since it is contrary to life. Thus it is said, "Last of all, the enemy, death, shall be destroyed."[437] This will be fulfilled at the resurrection: "He will transform the body of our lowliness, that it may be made like to the body of His glory."[438]

2. Because *kingdom* signifies the glory of Paradise. We pray, *Thy kingdom come* because *the kingdom of Heaven* signifies the glory of Paradise. This is easily understood. *Regnum* ("kingdom") is just another word for *regimen* ("government"), and the best government is one in which nothing is done against the will of the governor. Now, since God wills men to be saved, God's will is the salvation of mankind,[439] which will be realized most especially in Paradise, where there will be nothing contrary to man's salvation: "They shall gather out of His kingdom all scandals."[440]

In this world, however, there are many things contrary to the salvation of mankind. When, therefore, we pray *Thy kingdom come*, we ask to be made partakers of the heavenly kingdom and of the glory of Paradise.

Moreover, this kingdom is most desirable for three reasons:

[436] Amos 5:18.
[437] 1 Cor. 15:26.
[438] Phil. 3:21.
[439] 1 Tim. 2:4.
[440] Matt. 13:41.

a. Its supreme righteousness. It is desirable because of the supreme righteousness that obtains there: "Thy people shall be all righteous."[441] Here below the wicked are mingled with the good, whereas in Heaven there are no wicked and no sinners.

b. Its perfect liberty. This kingdom is desirable because of its perfect liberty. Although all men desire liberty naturally, here there is none; but in Heaven there is perfect liberty without any trace of bondage: "The creature itself will be delivered from the slavery of corruption."[442]

In fact, not only will all be free, but all will be kings: "Thou hast made us to our God a kingdom."[443] This is because all shall be of one will with God: whatever the saints will, God shall will; and whatever God wills, the saints shall will. Therefore, their will shall be done with God's will. In this way, all will reign, since the will of all will be done, and God shall be the crown of all: "In that day shall the Lord of hosts be for a crown of glory and for a diadem of beauty unto the residue of His people."[444]

c. Its wondrous wealth. This kingdom is also desirable because of its wondrous wealth: "The eye hath not seen, O God, besides Thee, what things Thou hast prepared for them that wait on Thee."[445] "Who satisfieth thy desire with good things."[446]

---

[441] Isa. 60:21.

[442] Rom. 8:21.

[443] Apoc. 5:10 (RSV = Rev. 5:10).

[444] Isa. 28:5.

[445] Isa. 64:4.

[446] Ps. 102:5 (RSV = Ps. 103:5).

Take note that whatever man seeks in this world, he will find it more perfect and more excellent in God alone.[447] If you seek delight, you will find supreme delight in God: "You shall see, and your heart shall rejoice."[448] "Everlasting joy shall be upon their heads."[449] Do you seek wealth? You will find in Him all you desire in abundance: "When the soul strays from Thee she seeks things apart from Thee, but finds all things impure and unprofitable until she returns to Thee."[450]

3. Because sometimes sin reigns in this world. We pray, *Thy kingdom come* because sometimes sin reigns in this world. This occurs when a man is so disposed that he follows at once the lure of sin and carries it into effect: "Let not sin reign in your mortal body"[451] but let God reign in your heart ("who says to Sion, 'Thy God shall reign' "[452]). This is when you are ready to obey God and keep all His commandments. Thus, when we ask that His kingdom may come, we pray that God (and not sin) may reign in us.

C. This fulfills the beatitude: "Blessed are the meek"
Thus, by this petition we shall obtain that beatitude[453] of which it is said: "Blessed are the meek."[454]

---

[447] *Summa Theologica*, I-II, Q. 69, art. 3, ad 3; II-II, Q. 89, art. 9, ad 3; Q. 121, art. 2.

[448] Isa. 66:14. This citation in the Vives edition is omitted in the Parma.

[449] Isa. 35:10. This citation in the Vives edition is omitted in the Parma.

[450] St. Augustine, *Confessions*, Bk. 2, ch. 6.

[451] Rom. 6:12.

[452] Isa. 52:7.

[453] *Summa Theologica*, I-II, Q. 69, art. 3, ad 3; II-II, Q. 89, art. 9, ad 3; Q. 121, art. 2.

[454] Matt. 5:4.

1. **Reliance on God.** According to the first explanation above [regarding our prayer that all may become subject to God], from the moment that a man desires God to be the Lord of all, he ceases to seek revenge for the injury done to himself and leaves that to God. For if you were to avenge yourself, you would no longer seek the advent of His kingdom.

2. **Detachment from earthly goods.** According to the second explanation above [regarding Heaven as the reign of God in the glory of Paradise], if you await the coming of His kingdom, i.e., the glory of Paradise, you have no need to regret the loss of earthly goods.

3. **Meekness.** And according to the third explanation above [regarding the reign of sin in this world], if you pray that God may reign in you, Christ who was most meek also will reign in you; and you will be meek in consequence: "Learn of me, for I am meek."[455] "Ye took joyfully the spoiling of your goods."[456]

[455] Matt. 11:29.
[456] Heb. 10:34.

VI

THY WILL BE DONE
ON EARTH AS IT IS IN HEAVEN
(Third Petition)

A. The gift of knowledge

Knowledge is the third gift bestowed on us by the Holy Spirit. For He bestows on the righteous not only the gift of fear and the gift of piety (which is a filial affection toward God, as already stated), but He also gives them wisdom. It is for this that David prayed: "Teach me goodness, discipline, and knowledge."[457] By this knowledge the Holy Spirit teaches us how to lead a good life.

Now, of all the signs of a man's knowledge and wisdom, none is proof of greater wisdom than that he does not cling to his own opinion: "Lean not upon thine own prudence."[458] For those who cling to their own judgment so as to mistrust others and trust in themselves alone invariably prove themselves fools and are judged as such. "Seest thou a man wise in his own conceit? There is more hope for a fool than for him."[459] But if a man distrusts his own judgment, that is a proof of his humility (which is why it is said, "Where humility is, there also is wisdom"[460]), whereas the proud are too self-confident.

---

[457] Ps. 118:66 (RSV = Ps. 119:66).
[458] Prov. 3:5.
[459] Prov. 26:12.
[460] Prov. 11:2.

Accordingly, we learn from the Holy Spirit (by His gift of knowledge) to do not our own but God's will, and by virtue of this gift we pray to God that His will may be done on earth as it is in Heaven. It is in this that the gift of knowledge is proved, so that when we say to God, *Thy will be done*, it is as when a sick man consults a physician. He takes the medicine not precisely because he wills it himself, but because it is the will of the physician. If he only took what he willed himself, he would be a fool.

Hence we should ask nothing of God but that His will be done in our regard (in other words, that His will be fulfilled in us). For man's heart is right when it agrees with the divine will. Christ did this: "I came down from Heaven to do, not my own will, but the will of Him that sent me."[461] For as God, Christ has the same will as the Father; but as man He has a distinct will from the Father and in respect of this will He says that He does not His own but His Father's will. For that reason He taught us to ask and pray, *Thy will be done*.

But how can this be explained in the face of the words of the Psalm: "He hath done whatsoever He hath willed"?[462] If He has done whatever He pleased in Heaven and on earth, what does He mean when He makes us say, *Thy will be done on earth as it is in Heaven?*

B. God's will for us

This is explained by observing that God wills three things in our regard, which we pray to be fulfilled:

1. Eternal life. God wills that we may have eternal life, because whoever makes a certain thing for a certain purpose wills that purpose for it. God made man, but not without a purpose, for as the Psalm says, "Hast Thou made all the children of men in

[461] John 6:38.
[462] Ps. 134:6 (RSV = Ps. 135:6).

vain?"[463] Therefore He made man for a certain purpose; but not for the sake of material pleasures, since dumb animals have them, but that he may have eternal life. For it is the Lord's will that man have eternal life.

When a thing attains the end for which it was made, it is said to be saved, whereas when it fails to reach that end it is said to be lost. Now, God made man for eternal life; and consequently, when man obtains eternal life, he is saved, which is God's will: "This is the will of my Father who sent me, that whosoever beholdeth the Son and believeth in Him, have eternal life."[464] This will is already fulfilled in the angels and saints, who are in Heaven, who see, know, and enjoy God.

But we desire that as God's will is fulfilled in the blessed who are in Heaven, even so may it be fulfilled in us who are on earth. This, then, is the sense of our prayer, *Thy will be done:* namely, that it be done in us who are on earth, even as it is fulfilled in the saints who are in Heaven.

2. Obedience to the Commandments. God wills that we keep His Commandments, because when we desire a particular thing, we do not only will what we desire, but we also will whatever enables us to obtain it. Thus a physician, in order to restore a man to health, also wills his diet, his medicine, and so on. Now, God wills us to obtain eternal life: "If thou wouldst enter life, keep the Commandments."[465]

Therefore He wills us to keep the Commandments: "Your reasonable service . . . so that ye find out what is the *good* and the *well-pleasing* and the *perfect* will of God."[466]

---

[463] Ps. 88:48 (RSV = Ps. 89:47).
[464] John 6:40.
[465] Matt. 19:17.
[466] Rom. 12:1, 2.

a. God's will is good: "Who teaches thee to profit."[467]

b. God's will is well-pleasing, and although displeasing to others, yet delightful to those who love His will: "Light is risen for the righteous and joy for the upright in heart."[468]

c. God's will is perfect: "Be ye perfect as also your heavenly Father is perfect."[469]

So when we say, *Thy will be done*, we pray that we may keep God's commandments; and this will of God is fulfilled in the righteous, but is not yet fulfilled in sinners. Now, the righteous are signified by *Heaven* and sinners by *earth*. Hence we pray that God's will be done on *earth*, i.e., in sinners, even as it is done in *Heaven*, i.e., in the righteous.

We must observe here that we have something to learn from the very manner of expression. For He does not say, *Do* or, *Let us do* but, *Thy will be done*. This is because two things are required in order to obtain eternal life: the grace of God and man's will. And although God made man without man's help, He does not sanctify him without his cooperation.

As St. Augustine says, "He who created thee without thyself, will not justify thee without thyself,"[470] because He wishes man to cooperate: "Turn ye unto me, and I will turn unto you."[471] "By the grace of God I am what I am, and His grace in me hath not been void."[472]

---

[467] Isa. 48:17.
[468] Ps. 96:11 (RSV = Ps. 97:11).
[469] Matt. 5:48.
[470] *Super Verb. Ap.*, serm. 15, commenting on John 14:12.
[471] Zach. 1:3.
[472] 1 Cor. 15:10.

Presume not therefore on yourself, but trust in the grace of God; nor be neglectful, but do your utmost.

Hence Christ does not say, *Let us do* (lest He seem to imply that God's grace counts for nothing); nor does He say, *Do* (lest He seem to state that man's will and effort are of no account). Rather he says, *Be it done* — by God's grace, with solicitude and effort on our part.

3. Restoration of the original dignity of man. God wills that man be restored to the state and dignity in which the first man was created, which was so great that his spirit and soul experienced no rebellion on the part of his flesh and sensuality. For as long as the soul was subject to God, the flesh was so subject to the spirit that it felt no corruption, whether of death or of sickness or of other passions.

But from the moment that the spirit and soul that stood between God and the flesh rebelled against God by sin, there and then the body rebelled against the soul. It began to be aware of death and infirmity, as well as of the ceaseless rebellion of sensuality against the spirit: "I behold another law in my members, warring against the law of my mind."[473] "The flesh lusteth against the spirit and the spirit against the flesh."[474]

Thus there is continual war between flesh and spirit, and man is ever being worsened by sin. Hence it is God's will that man be restored to his pristine state, namely, that the flesh be wholly delivered from all that rebels against the spirit: "This is the will of God, your sanctification."[475]

But this will of God cannot be fulfilled in this life, whereas it will be fulfilled at the resurrection of the saints, when bodies

[473] Rom. 7:23.
[474] Gal. 5:17.
[475] 1 Thess. 4:3.

will arise in glory and incorruption, and in a state of great perfection: "It is sown in dishonor; it shall rise in glory."[476] In the righteous, however, God's will is fulfilled with regard to the spirit by their righteousness, knowledge, and life. And therefore when we say, *Thy will be done*, we pray that this may be fulfilled also in the flesh. In this way we take *Heaven* to signify the spirit and *earth* to indicate the flesh. So the sense is, *Thy will be done on earth* (i.e., in our flesh) *as it is done in Heaven* (i.e., in our spirit) by righteousness.

C. This fulfills the beatitude: "Blessed are they who mourn"

By this petition we reach the blessedness of those who mourn, of which it is said: "Blessed are they who mourn, for they shall be comforted."[477] This applies to each of the three explanations given above:

1. Because eternal life is delayed. In accordance with the first explanation (above), we mourn because we desire eternal life, but it is delayed: "Woe is me that my sojourn is prolonged."[478] In fact, in the saints this longing is so great that because of it they desire death which in itself is repellent: "We have the courage even to prefer to be exiled from the body and to be at home with the Lord."[479]

2. Because keeping the Commandments is painful. In accordance with the second explanation (above), we mourn because we desire to keep the Commandments, yet, however sweet the Commandments are to the soul, they are bitter to the flesh,

[476] 1 Cor. 15:43.
[477] Matt. 5:5.
[478] Ps. 119:5 (RSV = Ps. 120:5-6).
[479] 2 Cor. 5:8.

which is continually buffeted: in the flesh, "going they went and wept," but in the soul, "coming they shall come with joy."[480]

3. Because flesh and spirit conflict. In accordance with the third explanation (above), we mourn because of the continual conflict between our flesh and our spirit [which frustrates our desire to be restored to the dignity of the first man], yet it is impossible for the soul not to be wounded at least by venial sins due to the flesh. This is why, until the soul is healed, it mourns: "Every night" (i.e., in the darkness of sin) "I will wash my bed" (i.e., my conscience).[481]

And they who weep thus reach their heavenly country, *to which may God bring us all.*

---

[480] Ps. 125:6, 7 (RSV = Ps. 126:6).
[481] Ps. 6:7 (RSV = Ps. 6:6).

VII

GIVE US THIS DAY OUR DAILY BREAD
(Fourth Petition)

A. The gift of fortitude

It often happens that one who is given great knowledge and wisdom is for that very reason disheartened, and so needs fortitude to hearten him lest he lack necessities. "It is He that giveth strength to the weary and increaseth force and might to them that are not."[482] It is the Holy Spirit who gives this fortitude: "The Spirit entered into me . . . and He set me upon my feet."[483] And this gift of fortitude prevents man's heart from fainting through fear of lacking necessities, and makes him trust without wavering that God will provide him with whatever he needs. For this reason the Holy Spirit, the giver of this fortitude, teaches us to pray to God to *give us this day our daily bread*. For this reason, He is called the "Spirit of fortitude."[484]

Observe here that in the first three petitions we ask for spiritual blessings that are begun in this life here below but are not perfected except in eternal life. So when we pray that God's name be hallowed, we ask that God's holiness be made known; when we pray that His kingdom may come, we ask that we be made partakers of

[482] Isa. 40:29.
[483] Ezek. 2:2.
[484] Isa. 11:2.

137

eternal life; and when we pray that His will be done, we ask that His will be fulfilled in us.

Although all these petitions begin to be fulfilled here below, they cannot be realized perfectly except in eternal life. Consequently, we need to pray for certain necessary things which can be had perfectly in the present life, and for this reason the Holy Spirit has taught us to ask for the needs of this present life. With these needs it is possible to be supplied perfectly here below, indicating at the same time that it is God who provides us with temporal goods. This is signified in the words, *Give us this day our daily bread.*

B. Sins that arise from desiring temporal goods

In these same words the Holy Spirit teaches us to avoid the sins which tend to arise from the desire for temporal goods:

1. **Greed.** The first is unbridled greed, whereby a man seeks things above his station and condition of life, being dissatisfied with those in keeping with it. For instance, if he is a common soldier, he wants to dress not as a soldier but as a nobleman; if he is an ordinary clergyman, he wishes to clothe himself not as a cleric but as a bishop. This vice draws a man away from spiritual goods, insofar as it makes him have an overwhelming desire for temporal things. Our Lord taught us to shun this vice by praying for bread only, i.e., the needs of the present life, each one according to his own station, which needs are expressed under the name of *bread.* Hence He did not teach us to ask for uncommon things, luxurious things, or a variety of things, but for bread, without which man cannot live, since it is the common need of all: "The chief thing for man's life is water and bread."[485] "Having food and clothing, with these we shall be content."[486]

[485] Ecclus. 29:27 (RSV = Sir. 29:21).
[486] 1 Tim. 6:8.

2. Fraud. The second vice consists in molesting and defrauding others in the acquisition of temporal goods. This vice is all the more fraught with danger since it is difficult to restore ill-gotten goods. For according to St. Augustine, "Unless a man restore what he has purloined, his sin is not forgiven."[487] Accordingly, we are taught here to shun this vice by asking for our own and not another's bread (since robbers eat not their own bread but another's).

3. Excessive solicitude. There are some who are never satisfied with what they have and always want more. This is lack of moderation, since desire should always be measured according to one's needs: "Give me neither beggary nor riches; give me but the necessities of life."[488] We are warned to avoid this vice in the words, *our daily bread,* that is to say, *the bread for one day or for one season.*

4. Voraciousness. This is the vice whereby some would devour in one day what would suffice for several days. These seek bread not for today but for ten days, and through being overly lavish, they waste all of it: "The drunkard and the glutton shall come to beggary."[489] "A workman that is a drunkard shall not be rich."[490]

5. Ingratitude. This is a great evil, since the ungrateful man prides himself on his wealth and fails to acknowledge that he owes all to God. Whatever we have, be it spiritual or temporal, comes from God: "All things are Thine and of Thine own have

[487] *Ep. ad Macedon,* 143.
[488] Prov. 30:8.
[489] Prov. 23:21.
[490] Ecclus. 19:1 (RSV = Sir. 19:1).

we given Thee."[491] Hence, in order to remove this vice, the Lord even says, *Give us our daily bread,* to remind us that all we have comes from God.

From this we learn a lesson. Sometimes a man has great wealth but derives no benefit from it, instead incurring loss both spiritual and temporal.

Some have perished through riches: "There is also another grievous evil which I have seen under the sun and that is common among men: a man to whom God hath given riches, wealth, and honor, so that his soul wanteth nothing at all that he desireth, yet God giveth him not power to eat thereof, but a stranger eateth it up."[492] And again: "Riches gathered together to the hurt of the owner."[493]

For this reason, we ought to pray that we may derive benefit from our wealth; and this we pray for when we say, *Give us our bread,* i.e., make our wealth profitable to us: "His bread in his belly shall be turned into the gall of asps within him. The riches which he hath swallowed he shall vomit up; God shall draw them out of his belly."[494]

6. Concern for worldly possessions. There are some who are worried from day to day about temporal matters as much as a year in advance. Those who are so concerned are never at rest: "Be not solicitous, saying: 'What shall we eat?' or 'What shall we drink?' or 'What are we to put on?' "[495] Hence our Lord teaches us to ask that our bread be given us *today,* i.e., whatever we need for the present.

[491] 1 Paralip. 29:14 (RSV = 1 Chron. 29:14).
[492] Eccles. 6:1, 2.
[493] Eccles. 5:12.
[494] Job 20:14, 15.
[495] Matt. 6:31.

C. The twofold meaning of *bread*

Moreover, we may discover in this bread another twofold meaning: the Sacramental Bread and the Bread of God's Word.

1. Sacramental Bread. Thus, we ask for our Sacramental Bread, which is prepared for us every day in the Church, praying that as we receive it sacramentally, so may it profit us unto salvation: "I am the living bread which came down from Heaven."[496] "He that eateth and drinketh unworthily eateth and drinketh judgment to himself."[497]

2. The Word of God. Again, this bread means the Word of God: "Not by bread alone doth man live but by every word that proceedeth from the mouth of God."[498] Hence we pray to Him to give us bread, that is to say, His Word. From this there arises in man the beatitude of hungering for righteousness, because the possession of spiritual goods increases our desire for them. This desire begets that hunger whose reward is the fullness of eternal life.

[496] John 6:51.
[497] 1 Cor. 11:29.
[498] Matt. 4:4.

VIII

AND FORGIVE US OUR TRESPASSES
AS WE FORGIVE THOSE WHO TRESPASS AGAINST US
(Fifth Petition)

A. The gift of counsel

There are, indeed, some possessed of great wisdom and fortitude who yet, being overconfident of their own powers, do not act wisely nor do they succeed in accomplishing what they intend: "Purpose is strengthened by counsel."[499] We must observe, however, that the Holy Spirit who gives strength also gives counsel, for every good counsel in the matter of man's spiritual welfare comes from the Holy Spirit.

Now, man needs counsel when he is in trouble, just as he needs to consult a physician when he is sick. So when his soul is sick through sin he must seek counsel in order to be healed. That the sinner needs counsel is indicated in the words of Daniel: "Let my counsel be acceptable unto thee, O King, and redeem thou thy sins with alms."[500] Hence, it is a very good counsel against sin that a man give alms and show mercy. For this reason the Holy Spirit teaches sinners to make this petition and to pray, *Forgive us our trespasses*.

We owe God that which we take away from His right, and God's right is that we do His will in preference to our own. Hence, we

[499] Prov. 20:18.
[500] Dan. 4:24.

deprive God of His right when we prefer our own will to His, and this is sin. Therefore sins are our debts, and the Holy Spirit counsels us to ask forgiveness of our sins. For this reason we say, *Forgive us our trespasses* [literally, *debts*].

Regarding these words, we may consider the following points: a) Why do we make this petition? b) When is it fulfilled? and c) What is required of us that it may be fulfilled?

B. Reasons for asking forgiveness

From this petition we gather two things that we need in this life:

1. That we may be ever fearful and humble, for there have been some so presumptuous as to assert that it is possible for man by his own powers to live here below without committing sin. But this has been given to none except Christ (who had the Spirit without measure) and the Blessed Virgin (who was full of grace, in whom there was no sin, and "of whom," St. Augustine says, "in the matter of sin, it is my wish to exclude all mention whatsoever"[501]).

To no other saint has this been granted without their incurring at least venial sin: "If we say that we have not sin, we deceive ourselves, and the truth is not in us."[502] This is confirmed by this fifth petition, for we cannot doubt that it is proper even for holy men to recite the Our Father, which includes the petition, *Forgive us our trespasses;* and, therefore, all acknowledge and confess themselves to be sinners or debtors. If, then, you are a sinner, you must be fearful and humble yourself.

2. That we should ever live in hope, for even though we are sinners, we must not despair, lest despair lead us to various and

[501] *De Nat. et Grat.*, 36.
[502] 1 John 1:8.

greater sins. Thus the Apostle says, "who despairing have given themselves over to licentiousness, unto the working of all uncleanness."[503] It is, therefore, most profitable for us to hope always, since however great a sinner a man may be, he should hope that God will forgive him if he is thoroughly contrite and converted. This hope is strengthened in us when we pray, *Forgive us our trespasses*.

The Novatians, however, destroyed this hope, for they said that those who sin once after being baptized never receive mercy. But this is not true, if Christ spoke the truth when He said, "I forgave thee all the debt because thou besoughtest me."[504] Consequently, whenever you ask for mercy you shall receive it, provided you ask with repentance for your sin.

Accordingly this petition gives rise to fear and hope, because every sinner who is contrite and confesses his sin receives mercy: and hence the need of this petition.

C. When is this petition fulfilled?

As regards the second point, we must observe that in sin there are two factors: the fault by which God is offended and the punishment due to the fault. The fault, however, is remitted through contrition which includes the intention of amendment and atonement: "I said: I will confess my transgressions unto the Lord; and Thou forgavest the iniquity of my sin."[505] Hence man must not despair, seeing that contrition together with the intention of confessing suffices for the forgiveness of sin.

Possibly someone will object, "If sins are forgiven when a man is contrite, why does he need a priest?" I reply that in contrition God forgives the fault and commutes eternal punishment into temporal;

[503] Eph. 4:19.
[504] Matt. 18:32.
[505] Ps. 31:5 (RSV = Ps. 32:5).

but the debt of temporal punishment remains.[506] Hence if a man were to die without confession — not because he refused it, but through being prevented — he would go to Purgatory, the punishment of which is very great, as St. Augustine says.

Accordingly, when you confess your sin, the priest absolves you from this punishment by the power of the keys to which you have submitted in confession. For this reason Christ said to His apostles, "Receive ye the Holy Spirit; whose sins ye shall forgive, they are forgiven them; and whose sins ye shall retain, they are retained."[507] Hence, if a man confesses once, some part of this punishment is taken away, and likewise when he confesses a second time. In fact, it may be that he confesses the sin so often that the whole punishment is remitted.

Moreover, the successors of the Apostles devised another means for the remission of this punishment, namely, the granting of indulgences[508] which avail those who are in a state of grace as much as is claimed for them and as indicated by the grantor. That the Pope can do this is sufficiently clear. For many are the good deeds of holy men who have never sinned, at least not mortally, which deeds were done for the common good of the Church. Likewise the merits of Christ and of the Blessed Virgin are, as it were, the Church's treasury. Thus the Sovereign Pontiff and those whom he delegates for the purpose, can allocate these merits wherever the need occurs. Consequently, sins are remitted not only as to their guilt by contrition, but also as to their punishment by confession and by indulgences.

D. What is required of us?

As regards the third point, we must observe that on our part we must forgive our neighbor his offenses against us, which is why it is

---

[506] *Summa Theologica*, Suppl., Q. 5, art. 2.
[507] John 20:22, 23.
[508] *Summa Theologica*, Suppl., Q. 25.

added, *As we forgive those who trespass against us.* Otherwise God would not forgive us: "Man to man reserveth anger; and doth he seek remedy of God?"[509] "Forgive and you shall be forgiven."[510] Thus this petition alone is made conditional, by our saying, *As we forgive those who trespass against us.* For if you do not forgive, you will not be forgiven.

You might say, "I will say the first part (*forgive us*) but I will omit what follows (*as we forgive those who trespass against us*)." Do you then seek to deceive Christ? Be sure that you do no such thing, since Christ, who made this prayer, remembers it well, and therefore He cannot be deceived. If, therefore, you say the words with your lips, fulfill them in your heart.

But someone may ask whether one who does not intend to forgive his neighbor, ought to say, *As we forgive those who trespass against us.* It seems not, since his words would be a lie. I answer that he does not lie, for he does not pray in his own person, but in that of the Church, who is not deceived; hence the petition is expressed in the plural.

Observe, however, that forgiveness is twofold. There is the forgiveness of those who are perfect, when he who is offended seeks out the offender: "Seek peace."[511] The other forgiveness applies to all in general — namely, that we forgive those who ask to be forgiven: "Forgive thy neighbor if he hath hurt thee, and then shall thy sins be forgiven thee when thou prayest."[512]

This leads us to another beatitude: *Blessed are the merciful,* for mercifulness makes us show mercy to our neighbor.

---

[509] Ecclus. 28:3 (RSV = Sir. 28:3).
[510] Luke 6:37.
[511] Ps. 33:15 (RSV = Ps. 34:14).
[512] Ecclus. 28:2 (RSV = Sir. 28:2).

AND LEAD US NOT INTO TEMPTATION
(Sixth Petition)

Some, although they have sinned, desire forgiveness of their sins and for this reason confess them and repent — yet they do not strive as much as they ought in order not to sin again. In this they are inconsistent: on the one hand they deplore their sins by repenting of them, while on the other hand, by sinning again they have more sins to deplore. Thus we read, "Wash yourselves, make yourselves clean, take away the evil of your devices from before my eyes, cease to do evil."[513] Hence, as stated above, Christ in the foregoing petition taught us to ask forgiveness of our sins, while in this petition He teaches us to ask that we may be able to avoid sin — that is, that we be not led into temptation and thus fall into sin: *And lead us not into temptation.*

Three questions arise here: a) What is temptation? b) How and by whom is man tempted? and c) How is he freed from temptation?

A. The nature of temptation
To tempt is nothing else but to try or to prove, so that to tempt a man is to prove his virtue.[514] Now, a man's virtue is tried or proven in two ways, corresponding to two things required by it. One

---

[513] Isa. 1:16.
[514] *Summa Theologica*, I, Q. 114, art. 2; II-II, Q. 97, art. 1.

requirement concerns doing good, in that virtue enables him to do good deeds; the other requirement is that he avoid evil: "Depart from evil and do good."[515] Accordingly a man's virtue is tried sometimes as regards his doing good, sometimes as regards his avoiding evil:

1. Regarding the doing of good. A man is sometimes tried in his readiness to do good deeds (for instance, to fast and the like) because your virtue is great when you are ready to do good. Thus God sometimes tempts a man, not that the man's virtue is unknown to Him, but that all may know it and take it as an example. In this way God tempted Abraham[516] and Job,[517] and it is thus that He often sends trials to the righteous, in order that by bearing trials in patience their virtue may be made manifest and they may themselves advance in virtue: "The Lord your God proveth you, that it may appear whether or not ye love Him."[518] Thus, God tempts man by inciting him to good deeds.

2. Regarding the doing of evil. A man's virtue is also tried by inducing him to evil deeds. If he offers strong resistance and does not consent, his virtue is great; whereas if he yields to the temptation, he is devoid of virtue. In this way no man is tempted by God, for as it is said, "God cannot be tempted to evil things; and Himself tempteth no man."[519]

B. The sources of temptation
Man is tempted by his own flesh, by the Devil, and by the world:

[515] Ps. 33:15 (RSV = Ps. 34:14).
[516] Gen. 22.
[517] Job 1.
[518] Deut. 13:3.
[519] James 1:13.

1. **The flesh tempts man** in two ways:

a. **The flesh instigates man to evil,** since it always seeks its own gratification — namely, carnal pleasures in which sin often occurs. For a man who indulges in carnal pleasures neglects spiritual things: "Everyone is tempted . . . by his own lust."[520]

b. **The flesh entices man from good,** for the spirit, for its own part, would always delight in spiritual goods, but the flesh encumbers and hinders the spirit: "The corruptible body is a load upon the soul."[521] "I delight in the law of God after the inward man, but I behold another law in my members, warring against the law of my mind and making me a captive to the law of sin which is in my members."[522] This temptation that comes from the flesh is most grievous since our foe, the flesh, is united to us; and as Boethius says, "No plague is more harmful than an enemy in the household." Therefore, we must be on the watch against it: "Watch and pray lest ye enter into temptation."[523]

2. **The Devil tempts man** with very great force, for even when the flesh is subdued, another tempter arises — the Devil, against whom we have a mighty struggle. Hence the Apostle says, "Our wrestling is not against flesh and blood, but against the principalities, against the powers, against the world-rulers of this darkness."[524] For this reason he is called significantly the Tempter:

[520] James 1:14.
[521] Wisd. 9:15.
[522] Rom. 7:22, 23.
[523] Matt. 26:41.
[524] Eph. 6:12.

"Lest haply the tempter hath tempted you."[525] In tempting he proceeds most cunningly. Like a skillful general about to besiege a fortified city, he seeks out the weak points in the object of his assault and tempts a man in those things in which he sees him to be weak. For this reason, he tempts him in those sins to which, after subduing his flesh, man is most inclined (for instance, to anger, pride, and other spiritual sins): "Your adversary the Devil goeth about as a roaring lion seeking to devour."[526]

The Devil tempts man in two ways:

a. The Devil deceives man: He does not at once suggest to man something that has an appearance of evil, but something that has a semblance of good. Thereby, at least in the beginning, he turns man from his chief purpose; afterward, it becomes easier for him to induce man to sin, once man has been turned ever so little from that purpose: "Even Satan disguiseth himself as an angel of light."[527]

b. The Devil enthralls man in his sin: Having led man on to sin, the Devil so enthralls him as to prevent him from arising out of sin: "The sinews of his testicles are wrapped together."[528] The devil, then, does two things: he deceives a man and after deceiving him, enchains him in his sin.

3. The world tempts man in two ways:

a. By awakening a desire for earthly goods. The world tempts man by awakening in him an excessive and unbridled

[525] 1 Thess. 3:5.
[526] 1 Pet. 5:8.
[527] 2 Cor. 11:14.
[528] Job 40:12.

desire for earthly goods. For this reason, the Apostle says that "the desire of money is the root of all evils."[529]

b. By threatening him with persecution. The world also tempts man by the threats of persecutors and tyrants: "We are wrapped up in darkness."[530] "All that would live piously in Christ Jesus shall suffer persecution."[531] "Fear not those that slay the body."[532]

Accordingly, it is now clear what temptation is and in what way and by whom man is tempted. We now have to see how man is to be freed from temptation.

C. Release from temptation

Here we must observe that Christ teaches us to pray, not that we may not be tempted but that we may not be *led into temptation* — for if man overcomes temptation he deserves a crown. Hence it is said, "Deem it all delight my brethren, when ye fall into diverse temptations" and "Son, when thou comest to the service of God . . . prepare thy soul for temptation."[533] Again: "Blessed is the man that is patient under temptation, for when he hath been proved he shall receive the crown of life."[534] Hence Christ teaches us to pray that we not be led into temptation by consenting to it. "Temptation hath not come upon you but such as man can bear,"[535] because to be tempted is human, but to consent is devilish.

[529] 1 Tim. 6:10.
[530] Job 37:19.
[531] 2 Tim. 3:12.
[532] Matt. 10:28.
[533] James 1:2; Ecclus. 2:1 (RSV = Sir. 2:1).
[534] James 1:12.
[535] 1 Cor. 10:13.

But does God lead a man to evil, so that we should say, *And lead us not into temptation?* I reply that God is said to lead us to evil by permitting us to do evil, to the extent that He withdraws His grace[536] from man by reason of his many sins, in consequence of which man falls into sin. For this reason we chant, "Forsake me not, O Lord, when my strength faileth."[537]

Yet He guides man by the fervor of charity, lest man be led into temptation, for the very least degree of charity is able to resist any sin whatever: "Many waters cannot quench charity."[538]

He also guides us by the light of our intelligence, by which He teaches us what to do. For, as the Philosopher says, everyone who sins is ignorant.[539] Thus we read, "I will give thee understanding and will instruct thee."[540] For this David prayed when he said, "Enlighten mine eyes lest I sleep in death; lest mine enemy say, I have prevailed against him."[541] This is imparted to us in the gift of understanding. Thus when we do not consent to temptation, we keep our hearts clean, of which it is said: "Blessed are the clean of heart, for they shall see God."[542]

It follows from this that this petition brings us to the sight of God, *to which may God lead us all.*

[536] *Summa Theologica,* I-II, Q. 70, art. 3.
[537] Ps. 70:9 (RSV = Ps. 71:9).
[538] Cant. 8:7 (RSV = Song of Sol. 8:7).
[539] *Ethics,* III, 1.
[540] Ps. 31:8 (RSV = Ps. 32:8).
[541] Ps. 12:4, 5 (RSV = Ps. 13:3, 4).
[542] Matt. 5:8.

X

BUT DELIVER US FROM EVIL
(Seventh Petition)

In the foregoing petitions, our Lord teaches us to seek forgiveness of our sins and how we may avoid temptations. In this petition, He bids us pray to be safeguarded from evils. This is a general petition against all evils (namely, sins, sickness, and afflictions, as St. Augustine says). Seeing, however, that mention has already been made of sin and temptation, it remains for other evils to be mentioned (namely, the trials and afflictions of this world), from which God delivers us in four ways:

A. God prevents evils

God prevents the occurrence of evils, but He does not do this often, since the saints are afflicted in this world and since "everyone who would live piously in Christ Jesus shall suffer persecution."[543] Yet sometimes God does prevent a man from being afflicted by an evil — namely, when He knows him to be unable to bear it (just as a physician does not apply violent remedies to a weak patient): "Behold I have set before thee an open door, and no man can shut it, for thou hast little strength."[544] In Heaven, however, this will apply to all, seeing that there none will be afflicted: "He shall deliver

---

[543] 2 Tim. 3:12.

[544] Apoc. 3:8 (RSV = Rev. 3:8).

155

thee in six troubles" (those, that is, of the present life, which is divided into six stages) "and in the seventh, evil shall not touch thee."[545] "They shall hunger no more, neither thirst any more."[546]

B. God comforts the suffering

He delivers us from afflictions when He comforts us in them. For unless He comforts us, we cannot endure: "We were utterly weighed down beyond our strength."[547] "God who comforteth the humble, comforteth us."[548] "According to the multitude of my sorrows in my heart, Thy comforts delight my soul."[549]

C. God rewards the afflicted

He bestows so many blessings on those who are afflicted that their evils are forgotten: "After the storm Thou makest it calm."[550] Hence such afflictions and trials are not to be feared, since they are easy to bear both on account of the attendant consolations and because of their short duration: "Our present light affliction ever more and more abundantly worketh out for us an eternal weight of glory,"[551] because by means thereof we obtain eternal life.

D. God strengthens men through trials

He delivers us from evil insofar as temptations and trials are conducive to our profit. Thus He does not say, *Deliver us from trials*, but *from evil*, because trials bring the saints a crown, and for that reason they glory in their trials. Thus the Apostle says, "And not

[545] Job 5:19.
[546] Apoc. 7:16 (RSV = Rev. 7:16).
[547] 2 Cor. 1:8.
[548] Cf. 2 Cor. 7:6.
[549] Ps. 93:19 (RSV = Ps. 94:19).
[550] Tob. 3:22.
[551] 2 Cor. 4:17.

only so, but we exult in our tribulations also, knowing that tribulation worketh patience."[552] "In time of tribulation Thou forgivest sins."[553]

Thus God delivers man from evil and from trials by turning them to man's profit, which is a sign of very great wisdom, because it is a mark of wisdom to direct evil to a good purpose (and this is the result of patience in bearing trials).

Other virtues indeed employ good things, but patience profits by evil things, which is why it is necessary only in evils, i.e., in adversity: "The learning of a man is known by his patience."[554]

Hence the Holy Spirit by means of the gift of wisdom makes us pray this way, so that we may obtain the beatitude which is the reward of peace. For by patience we obtain peace whether times be good or evil. For this reason, peacemakers are called the children of God because they are like God: just as nothing can hurt God, so nothing can harm them, whether they prosper or suffer. Therefore, "Blessed are the peacemakers, for they shall be called the children of God."[555]

Amen. This is said to ratify all the petitions.

---

[552] Rom. 5:3.
[553] Tob. 3:13.
[554] Prov. 19:11.
[555] Matt. 5:9.

XI

A SHORT EXPOSITION OF THE LORD'S PRAYER

By way of summing up what has been said, observe that the Lord's Prayer contains what we ought to desire and what we ought to avoid:[556]

A. What men should desire

1. **The glory of God.** Of all desirable things the first place belongs to that which is most lovable. This is God, and therefore you seek first the glory of God by saying, *Hallowed be Thy name.*

Concerning yourself, you should desire from God:

2. **Eternal life.** For this you pray by saying, *Thy kingdom come.*

3. **Fulfillment of God's will and His justice.** For this you ask by saying, *Thy will be done on earth as it is in Heaven.*

4. **The necessities of life.** For this you pray by saying, *Give us this day our daily bread.*

[556] *Summa Theologica,* II-II, Q. 83, art. 9.

Of these [things you should desire for yourself] our Lord says, "Seek ye first the kingdom of God" (as regards the first); "and His justice" (as regards the second); "and all these things shall be added unto you" (as regards the third).[557]

B. What men should avoid
The things to be avoided and fled from are those which are incompatible with the fourfold good (indicated above):

1. Evil, which cannot destroy the glory of God: "If thou sin, what shalt thou hurt Him? If thou be righteous what givest thou Him?"[558] For the evil with which He punishes and the good with which He rewards redound to God's glory.

2. Sin, which is contrary to eternal life, because by sin eternal life is lost. Therefore, to remove this evil we say, *Forgive us our trespasses as we forgive those who trespass against us.*

3. Temptations, which are opposed to righteousness and good works, since temptations hinder us from performing good works. To remove this evil, we pray, *And lead us not into temptation.*

4. Troubles and trials, which are opposed to all those goods that we need.

To remove these evils we pray, *But deliver us from evil. Amen.*

[557] Matt. 6:33.
[558] Job 35:6, 7.

XII

THE HAIL MARY,
OR THE "ANGELIC SALUTATION"

This salutation is divided into three parts. The first contains the words of the angel: *Hail, full of grace, the Lord is with thee. Blessed art thou among women.*[559] The second part is composed of the words of Elizabeth, mother of John the Baptist: *Blessed is the fruit of thy womb.*[560] The third part (namely, *Mary*) was added by the Church, for the angel did not say, *Hail, Mary*, but, *Hail, full of grace*. But because of its meaning, the name *Mary* is in keeping with the angel's words, as will be made plain.

HAIL MARY

A. The superiority of angels over men

With regard to the first part, we must observe that in earlier times it was no small event when angels appeared to men, or men paid reverence to them, such a thing being recorded as deserving of great praise. Hence it is mentioned in praise of Abraham that he gave hospitality to angels and paid them reverence.

But it was unheard of that an angel should show reverence to a human being until one of them greeted the Blessed Virgin reverently,

[559] Luke 1:28.
[560] Luke 1:42.

saying, *Hail.* In ancient times, reverence was shown by men to angels, but not by angels to men, because angels are greater than man in three respects:

1. In dignity. An angel surpasses man in dignity, since an angel is of a spiritual nature ("who maketh His angels spirits"[561]), whereas man is of a corruptible nature. For this reason Abraham said, "I will speak to my Lord, whereas I am dust and ashes."[562] Hence it was not fitting that a spiritual and incorruptible creature should show reverence toward a corruptible one, namely, man.

2. In close association with God. An angel surpasses man in familiar association with God, being a member of God's household and standing by His throne: "Thousands of thousands ministered to Him, and ten thousand times a hundred thousand stood before Him."[563] Man, on the other hand, is like a stranger and far away from God on account of sin: "I have wandered afar off."[564] Thus it is fitting that man should revere an angel, who is intimate and familiar with the King.

3. In the fullness of divine grace. An angel surpasses man in the fullness of the splendor of divine grace, since an angel partakes of the divine light in the greatest plenitude: "Is there any number of His armies? And upon whom doth not His light arise?"[565] For this reason angels always appear surrounded by light. Men, on the other hand, although they partake somewhat of this

---

[561] Ps. 103:4 (RSV = Ps. 104:4).
[562] Gen. 18:27.
[563] Dan. 7:10.
[564] Ps. 54:8 (RSV = Ps. 55:7).
[565] Job 25:3.

same light of grace, have but a small share of it which is not without some darkness.

So it was not fitting that an angel should pay respect to a man until one should be found in human nature who would surpass the angels in these three ways — and such was the Blessed Virgin. Thus, in order to show that she excelled him, the angel desired to show her reverence by saying, *Hail*.

B. The superiority of the Blessed Virgin over the angels
Accordingly, the Blessed Virgin surpasses the angels in these three respects:

FULL OF GRACE

1. In dignity. She surpasses the angels in her fullness of grace, which is greater in her than in any angel. To indicate this, the angel paid reverence to her by saying *full of grace*, as if to say, "I bow to thee because thou dost surpass me in fullness of grace."

The Blessed Virgin was said to be full of grace in three respects:

a. Grace filled her soul. She was full of grace as regards her soul, in which dwelt all the plenitude of grace. For God's grace is given for two purposes: the performance of good deeds and the avoidance of evil.

As regards both, the Blessed Virgin received grace in the most perfect degree, since after Christ she was free from sin more than any other saint. For sin is either original — and from this she was cleansed in the womb[566] — or mortal or

---

[566] In contrast to the position St. Thomas holds in this article, the Church solemnly declared in 1854 that Mary is the Immaculate Conception, i.e., not merely *born* without the stain of Original Sin but also *conceived* without it.

venial, from which she was free. Thus it is said: "Thou art all fair, O my love; and there is not a spot in thee."[567] And St. Augustine says, "Except the holy Virgin Mary, if all the saints (both men and women) while living here below had been asked whether they were without sin, all would have cried aloud with one voice: 'If we say that we have no sin, we deceive ourselves and the truth is not in us'[568] — except I repeat, this holy Virgin, about whom, for our Lord's honor, I wish to exclude all mention whatsoever in the matter of sin. For we know that an abundance of grace was given her that she might be in every way the conqueror of sin, seeing that she conceived and brought forth Him who most certainly was guilty of no sin."[569]

But Christ surpassed the Blessed Virgin in that He was conceived and born without Original Sin, whereas the Blessed Virgin was conceived but not born in Original Sin. She practiced the works of *all* the virtues, while other saints were conspicuous in certain particular virtues — one for humility, another for chastity, another for mercy — for which reason each one is an example to us of some special virtue. (Thus, for instance, St. Nicholas is an example of mercy, and so on.)

But the Blessed Virgin is an example of *all* virtues. Thus you find in her a model of humility ("Behold the handmaid of the Lord,"[570] and further on, "He hath regarded the humility of His handmaid"[571]); of chastity ("Because I know not

---

[567] Cant. 4:7 (RSV = Song of Sol. 4:7).

[568] 1 John 1:8.

[569] *De Nat. et Grat.*, 36; cf. St. Thomas Aquinas, *Summa Theologica*, III, Q. 30, art. 4.

[570] Luke 1:38.

[571] Luke 1:48.

man"[572]); and of all other virtues, as can easily be shown. Therefore, the Blessed Virgin was full of grace both in performing good works and in avoiding evil deeds.

b. Grace overflowed into her body. The Blessed Virgin was full of grace as regards the overflow of grace from her soul into her flesh, or body. For while it is a great thing in the saints to be so endowed with grace that their souls are holy, the soul of the Blessed Virgin was so full of grace that it overflowed into her flesh, fitting it for the conception of God's Son.[573] Thus Hugh of St. Victor says, "The Holy Spirit had so kindled in her heart the fire of divine love that it worked wonders in her flesh, yea, even so that she gave birth to God made man." And St. Luke says, "For the Holy One that shall be born of thee shall be called the Son of God."[574]

c. Grace overflows from her onto all mankind. So full of grace was the Blessed Virgin, that it overflows onto all mankind. It is, indeed, a great thing that any one saint has so much grace that it is conducive to the salvation of many; but it is most wondrous to have so much grace as to suffice for the salvation of all mankind. Thus it is in Christ and in the Blessed Virgin. So in every danger you can find a refuge in this same glorious Virgin: "A thousand bucklers" (i.e., protections from peril) "hang therefrom."[575] Likewise, you may obtain her assistance in every virtuous deed: "In me is all hope of life and of virtue."[576]

[572] Luke 1:34.
[573] *Summa Theologica*, II, Q. 31, art. 4, 5.
[574] Luke 1:35.
[575] Cant. 4:4 (RSV = Song of Sol. 4:4).
[576] Ecclus. 24:25 (No equivalent in RSV).

She is, therefore, full of grace, surpassing the angels in that plenitude. For this reason she is rightly called Mary, which signifies that in herself she is enlightened ("The Lord will fill thy soul with brightness"[577]) and that she enlightens others throughout the world. Thus, she is compared to the sun and to the moon.

THE LORD IS WITH THEE

1. In her close association with God. The Blessed Virgin surpasses the angels in her familiar association with God. To indicate this the angel said, *The Lord is with thee,* as if to say, "I bow to thee because thou art more familiar with God than I am, seeing that the Lord is with thee."

a. In her relation to God the Father: "The Lord," he said (i.e., the Father whose Son is also thy Son) — which cannot be said of any angel or of any creature whatever: "For the Holy One who shall be born of thee shall be called the Son of God."

b. In her relation to God the Son: The Lord God the Son was in her womb: "Rejoice and praise, O thou dwelling of Sion, for great is he that is in the midst of thee, the Holy One of Israel."[578]

So the Lord is with the Blessed Virgin in a different manner than with an angel. With her, He is as her Son; with the angel, as his Lord.

c. In her relation to God the Holy Spirit: The Lord God the Holy Spirit was with her as in a temple. So we say, "Temple

[577] Isa. 58:11.
[578] Isa 12:6.

166

of the Lord, sanctuary of the Holy Spirit,"[579] because she conceived of the Holy Spirit.[580] "The Holy Spirit shall come upon thee."[581]

In these ways, the Blessed Virgin is more intimately associated with God than an angel is, since with her are God the Father, God the Son, and God the Holy Spirit — in a word, the whole Trinity. Hence the words of the chant: "Throne wherein the three Divine Persons recline."[582] So no greater praise could be addressed to her than that which is found in the words, *The Lord is with thee*.

She also deserved to be so reverenced by the angel, in that being the Mother of our Lord she is our Lady. Consequently, she is fittingly named *Mary*, which in the Syrian tongue means "lady."

BLESSED ART THOU AMONG WOMEN

3. In the fullness of divine grace. The Blessed Virgin excels the angels in purity, because not only was she pure in herself, but she obtains purity for others. In fact, she was most pure, being immune both from sin (she was free from mortal and venial sin) and from punishment.

For a triple curse befell mankind on account of sin:

a. Mary was immune from the curse on woman. The first curse fell on woman: namely, that she would conceive in

---

[579] Antiphon, *Beata Dei Genitrix* from the *Little Office of Our Lady*.

[580] *Summa Theologica*, III, Q. 32.

[581] Luke 1:35.

[582] *Totius Trinitatis Nobile Triclinium*.

corruption, bear with weariness, and bring forth in pain.[583] But the Blessed Virgin was immune from these, since she conceived without corruption, bore with ease, and gave birth with joy to our Savior: "It shall bud forth and blossom and shall rejoice and praise."[584]

b. She was immune from the curse on man. The second curse was pronounced on man: namely, that he should earn his bread by the sweat of his brow.[585] The Blessed Virgin was free from this, since as the Apostle says, a virgin is free from care for the things of this world and gives her mind to God alone.[586]

c. She was immune from the curse on man *and* woman. The third curse fell upon both man and woman: that they would return to dust. From this also was the Blessed Virgin exempt, since she was taken up bodily into Heaven, for we believe that after her death she was raised up and carried into Heaven: "Arise, O Lord, into Thy rest: Thou and the ark which Thou didst sanctify."[587]

Accordingly she was free from every curse, and therefore, was *blessed among women*, since she alone lifted the curse, brought us a blessing, and opened the gates of Heaven. Thus is the name *Mary* proper to her, which means "star of the sea." (Just as the star of the sea guides sailors to port, so Mary guides Christ's followers to heavenly glory.)

---

[583] *Summa Theologica*, II-II, Q. 164, art. 2.
[584] Isa. 35:2.
[585] Gen. 3:19.
[586] 1 Cor. 7:34.
[587] Ps. 131:8 (RSV = Ps. 132:8).

AND BLESSED IS THE FRUIT OF THY WOMB

C. Only the Virgin's Fruit affords what Eve sought in her fruit
The sinner at times seeks but does not find, whereas the righteous seeks and finds: "The wealth of the sinner is laid up for the just."[588] Thus Eve sought the fruit [of the tree], but did not find in it all that she coveted; whereas the Blessed Virgin in her Fruit found all that Eve had desired:

1. Likeness to God. In her fruit, Eve sought to become like gods, knowing good and evil (which the Devil falsely promised). "Ye shall be as gods," said the liar.[589] Thus he lied, for "he is a liar, and the father of lies."[590] For through eating the fruit, Eve did not become like God, but unlike Him, since by sinning she turned away from God, her salvation, and was expelled from Paradise.

On the other hand, the Blessed Virgin found likeness to God in the Fruit of her womb — and so do all followers of Christ — since through Christ we are united and likened to God. "When He shall appear, we shall be like unto Him, for we shall see Him as He is."[591]

2. Delight. Eve in her fruit sought pleasure, since it was good to eat; yet she did not find it, for at once she perceived that she was naked, and tasted sorrow. But in the Fruit of the Blessed Virgin we find sweetness and salvation. "He that eateth my flesh . . . hath eternal life."[592]

[588] Prov. 13:22.
[589] Gen. 3:5.
[590] John 8:44.
[591] 1 John 3:2.
[592] John 6:55 (RSV = John 6:54).

3. Beauty. Eve in her fruit sought beauty: Eve's fruit was fair to the eyes. Yet fairer still is the Virgin's Fruit, on whom the angels long to gaze: "Thou art fairer than the sons of men."[593] This is because He is the "brightness of the Father's glory."[594] Accordingly, Eve could not find in her fruit that which no sinner can find in his sin.

Therefore, let us seek in the Virgin's Fruit that which we desire to have. This Fruit is blessed by God, because God so filled Him with all grace that it overflows upon us who bow to Him in adoration: "Blessed be the God and Father of our Lord Jesus Christ, who hath blessed us with every spiritual blessing on high in Christ."[595] He is blessed by the angels: "Blessing and glory and wisdom and thanksgiving and honor and power and might be to our God forever and ever."[596] And He is blessed by men: "Let every tongue confess that our Lord Jesus Christ is in the glory of God the Father."[597] "Blessed is He who comes in the name of the Lord."[598]

Thus is the Virgin blessed, but still more blessed is her Fruit.

[593] Ps. 44:3 (RSV = Ps. 45:2).
[594] Heb. 1:3.
[595] Eph. 1:3.
[596] Apoc. 7:12 (RSV = Rev. 7:12).
[597] Phil. 2:11.
[598] Ps. 117:26 (RSV = Ps. 118:26).

Part 3

How Christians Should Live

The Commandments

THE COMMANDMENTS[599]

1. Thou shalt not have strange gods before me.

2. Thou shalt not take the name of the Lord thy God in vain.

3. Remember that thou keep holy the Sabbath day.

4. Honor thy father and thy mother.

5. Thou shalt not kill.

6. Thou shalt not commit adultery.

7. Thou shalt not steal.

8. Thou shalt not bear false witness against thy neighbor.

9. Thou shalt not covet thy neighbor's goods.

10. Thou shalt not covet thy neighbor's wife.

---

[599] Exod. 20:2-17 and Deut. 5:6-21 list all the Commandments. St. Thomas places the Tenth Commandment (in the present traditional enumeration) before the Ninth. The Tenth Commandment is wider in extension than the Ninth, which is specific.

I

THOU SHALT NOT HAVE
STRANGE GODS BEFORE ME

The First Commandment which relates to the love of God is: *Thou shalt not have strange gods before me*. For an understanding of this commandment, we must know how it was violated in earlier times.

A. How the First Commandment was violated

1. Some people worshiped demons: "All the gods of the Gentiles are devils."[600] This is the greatest and most detestable of all sins. Even now there are many who transgress this commandment, such as those who practice divinations and fortunetelling. Such things, according to St. Augustine, cannot be done without some kind of pact with the Devil. "I would not that you should be made partakers with devils."[601]

2. Some worshiped the heavenly bodies, believing the stars to be gods: "They have imagined the sun and the moon to be the gods that rule the world."[602] For this reason Moses forbade the Jews to raise their eyes or adore the sun, moon, and stars: "Keep

[600] Ps. 95:5 (RSV = Ps. 96:5).
[601] 1 Cor. 10:20.
[602] Wisd. 13:2.

173

therefore your souls carefully . . . lest perhaps lifting up thine eyes to heaven, thou see the sun, the moon, and all the stars of heaven, and being deceived by error, thou adore and serve them which the Lord thy God created for the service of all the nations."[603] The astrologers sin against this commandment in that they say that these bodies are the rulers of souls, when in truth they were made for the use of man, whose sole ruler is God.

3. Some worshiped the lower elements: "They imagined the fire or the wind . . . to be gods."[604] Into this error also fall those who wrongly use the things of this earth and love them too much: "covetous persons (who serve idols)."[605]

4. Some worshiped their ancestors (for three reasons):

a. From their carnal nature
"For a father being afflicted with a bitter grief made to himself the image of his son who was quickly taken away; and him who then had died as a man, he began now to worship as a god, appointing him rites and sacrifices among his servants."[606]

b. Because of flattery
Being unable to worship certain men in their presence, they, bowing down, honored them in their absence by making statues of them and worshiping one for the other: "whom they had a mind to honor . . . they made an image . . . that they might honor as present him that was absent."[607] Of such

[603] Deut. 4:15, 19.
[604] Wisd. 13:2.
[605] Eph. 5:5.
[606] Wisd. 14:15.
[607] Wisd. 14:17.

also are those men who love and honor other men more than God: "He that loveth his father and mother more than me is not worthy of me."[608] "Put your trust not in princes nor in the children of man, in whom there is no salvation."[609]

c. From presumption
Some, because of their presumption, had themselves called gods. Such, for example, was Nebuchadnezzar.[610] "Thy heart is lifted up and thou hast said, 'I am God.' "[611]

d. From desire for pleasure
Such also are those who believe more in their own pleasures than in the precepts of God. They worship themselves as gods, for by seeking the pleasures of the flesh, they worship their own bodies instead of God: "Their god is their belly."[612] We must therefore avoid all these things.

B. Reasons we should adore one God
As we have already said, the First Commandment forbids us to worship other than the one God: *Thou shalt not have strange gods before me*. There are five reasons for this:

1. God's dignity
The first reason is the dignity of God, which, were it belittled in any way, would be an injury to God. We see something similar to this in the customs of men. Reverence is due to every degree of dignity. Thus, a traitor to the king is he who robs him of what

608 Matt. 10:37.
609 Ps. 145:2-3 (RSV = Ps. 146:3).
610 Jth. 3:13 (RSV = Jth. 3:8).
611 Ezek. 28:2.
612 Phil. 3:19.

he ought to maintain. Such, too, is the conduct of some toward God: "They changed the glory of the incorruptible God into the likeness of the image of a corruptible man."[613]

This is highly displeasing to God: "I will not give my glory to another, nor my praise to graven things."[614] For it must be known that the dignity of God consists in His omniscience, since the name of God (*Deus*) is from "seeing"; and this is one of the signs of divinity: "Show the things that are to come hereafter, and we shall know that ye are gods."[615] "All things are naked and open to His eyes."[616] But this dignity of God is denied Him by practitioners of divination, and of them it is said: "Should not the people seek of their God? Should they consult the dead on behalf of the living?"[617]

2. God's bounty

We also should worship only God because we receive every good from Him. This also is of the dignity of God, that He is the maker and giver of all good things: "When Thou openest Thy hand, they shall all be filled with good."[618] And this is implied in the name of God (*Deus*), which is said to be "distributor" (that is, *dator*) of all things, because He fills all things with His goodness. You are indeed ungrateful if you do not appreciate what you have received from Him and, furthermore, if you make for yourself another god as the sons of Israel made an idol after they had been brought out of Egypt: "I will go after my lovers."[619]

---

[613] Rom. 1:23.
[614] Isa. 42:8.
[615] Isa. 41:23.
[616] Heb. 4:13.
[617] Isa. 8:19.
[618] Ps. 103:28 (RSV = Ps. 104:28).
[619] Osee 2:5 (RSV = Hos. 2:5).

We do this also when we put too much trust in someone other than God, such as may occur when we seek help from another: "Blessed is the man whose hope is in the name of the Lord."[620] Thus the Apostle says: "Now, that you have known God . . . how can you turn again to the weak and needy elements? . . . You observe days and months and times and years."[621]

3. The strength of our promise

The third reason we should worship the one God is taken from our solemn promise. For we have renounced the Devil, and we have promised fidelity to God alone. This is a promise which we cannot break: "A man making void the Law of Moses dieth without mercy under two or three witnesses. How much more think ye he deserveth punishment who hath trodden underfoot the Son of God, hath esteemed unclean the blood of the testament by which he was sanctified, and hath offered an affront to the Spirit of grace?"[622] "Whilst her husband liveth, she shall be called an adulteress, if she be with another man."[623] Woe, then, to the sinner who enters the land by two ways and who "halts between two sides."[624]

4. The terrible burden of serving the Devil

The fourth reason we should worship the one God is because of the great burden that is imposed on us by service to the Devil: "You shall serve strange gods day and night, who will give you no rest."[625] The Devil is not satisfied with leading us to one sin,

---

[620] Ps. 39:5 (RSV = Ps. 40:4).
[621] Gal. 4:9, 10.
[622] Heb. 10:28-29.
[623] Rom. 7:3.
[624] 3 Kings 18:21 (RSV = 1 Kings 18:21).
[625] Jer. 16:13.

but tries to lead us on to others: "whosoever sins shall be a slave of sin."[626] It is, therefore, not easy for us to escape from the habit of sin. Thus St. Gregory says: "The sin which is not remitted by penance soon draws man into another sin."[627] The very opposite of all this is true of service to God, for His commandments are not a heavy burden: "My yoke is sweet, and my burden is light."[628] A person is considered to have done enough if he does for God as much as he has done for the sake of sin: "For as you have yielded your members unto iniquity to serve uncleanness and iniquity, so now yield your members to serve justice unto sanctification."[629] But on the contrary, it is written of those who serve the Devil: "We wearied ourselves in the way of iniquity and destruction and have walked through hard ways."[630] And again: "They have labored to commit iniquity."[631]

5. The greatness of the reward

The fifth reason we should worship the one God is taken from the greatness of the reward or prize. In no law are such rewards promised as in the law of Christ. To the Mohammedans are promised rivers flowing with milk and honey; to the Jews, the Promised Land; but to Christians, the glory of the angels: "They shall be as the angels of God in Heaven."[632] It was with this in mind that St. Peter asked: "Lord, to whom shall we go? Thou hast the words of eternal life."[633]

---

[626] John 8:34.
[627] St. Gregory the Great, *Homily 11 on Ezekiel*, 24.
[628] Matt. 11:30.
[629] Rom. 6:19.
[630] Wisd. 5:7.
[631] Jer. 9:5.
[632] Matt. 22:30.
[633] John 6:69 (RSV = John 6:68).

II

THOU SHALT NOT TAKE THE NAME
OF THE LORD THY GOD IN VAIN

This is the Second Commandment of the Law. Just as there is but one God we must worship, so there is but one God we should revere in a special manner. This, first of all, has reference to the name of God: *Thou shalt not take the name of the Lord thy God in vain.*

A. The meanings of *in vain*

1. *Vain* can mean "false"
"They have spoken vain things every one to his neighbor."[634] Therefore, we take the name of God in vain when we use it to confirm that which is not true: "Love not a false oath."[635] "Thou shalt not live because thou hast spoken a lie in the name of the Lord."[636] Anyone so doing injures God, himself, and all men.

a. Falsehood insults God
It is an insult to God because, when you swear by God, you call Him to witness; and when you swear falsely, you either believe God to be ignorant of the truth (and thus you ascribe

[634] Ps. 11:3 (RSV = Ps. 12:2).
[635] Zach. 8:17.
[636] Zach. 13:3.

ignorance to God, whereas "all things are naked and open to His eyes"[637]) or you think that God loves a lie, whereas He hates it: "Thou wilt destroy all that speak a lie."[638] Or, again, you detract from His power, as if He were not able to punish a lie.

b. Falsehood injures the teller
Likewise, he who swears falsely injures himself, for he binds himself to the judgment of God. To say, "By God, this is so," is the same as to say, "May God punish me if it is not so!"

c. Falsehood injures others
Finally, he who swears falsely injures other men. For there can be no lasting society unless men believe one another. Matters that are doubtful may be confirmed by oaths: "An oath in confirmation puts an end to all controversy."[639]

Therefore, he who violates this precept injures God, is cruel to himself, and harms other men.

2. Vain can mean "useless"
"The Lord knoweth the thoughts of men, that they are vain."[640] Therefore, God's name is taken in vain when it is used to confirm things needlessly.

In the Old Law it was forbidden to swear falsely: "Thou shalt not take the name of the Lord thy God in vain."[641] And Christ forbade the taking of oaths except in case of necessity:

[637] Heb. 4:13.
[638] Ps. 5:7 (RSV = Ps. 5:6).
[639] Heb. 6:16.
[640] Ps. 93:11 (RSV = Ps. 94:11).
[641] Deut. 5:11.

"You have heard that it was said to them of old, 'Thou shalt not forswear thyself. . . .' But I say to you, do not swear at all."[642] And the reason is that in no part of our body are we so weak as in the tongue, for "the tongue no man can tame."[643] Thus, even in light matters we can perjure ourselves. "Let your speech be: 'Yea, yea; no, no.' . . . But I say to you, do not swear at all."[644]

Note well that an oath is like medicine, which is never taken continually but only in times of necessity. Hence the Lord adds: "And that which is over and above these is evil."[645] "Let not the mouth be accustomed to swearing, for in it there are many falls. And let not the name of God be usual in thy mouth, and meddle not with the names of saints. For thou shalt not escape free from them."[646]

3. Vain can signify "sin" or "injustice"

"O ye sons of men, how long will you be dull of heart? Why do you love vanity?"[647] Therefore, he who swears that he will commit a sin takes the name of his God in vain. Justice consists in doing good and avoiding evil. Therefore, if you take an oath that you will steal or commit some crime of this sort, you sin against justice. And although you must not keep this oath, you are still guilty of perjury. Herod did this against John.[648] It is likewise against justice when a person swears *not* to do some good act, as not to enter a church or a religious community.

---

[642] Matt. 5:33-34.
[643] James 3:8.
[644] Matt. 5:37, 34.
[645] Matt. 5:37.
[646] Ecclus. 23:9-10 (RSV = Sir. 23:9-10).
[647] Ps. 4:3 (RSV = Ps. 4:2).
[648] Mark 6:17-27.

And although this oath, too, is not binding, yet, despite this, the person himself is a perjurer.

B. Taking God's name in vain

1. False oaths

A person cannot, therefore, swear to a falsehood, swear without good reason, or in any way swear against justice: "And thou shalt swear, 'As the Lord liveth,' in truth, in judgment, and in justice."[649]

2. Foolish oaths

Sometimes *vain* also means "foolish": "All men are vain in whom there is not the knowledge of God."[650] Accordingly, he who by blasphemy takes the name of God foolishly, takes the name of God in vain: "And he that blasphemeth the name of the Lord, dying let him die."[651]

C. Taking God's name justly

Thou shalt not take the name of the Lord thy God in vain. However, the name of God may be taken justly for six purposes.

1. To confirm something that is said (as in an oath), we may take God's name justly. In doing this, we show that God alone is the first truth, and we also show due reverence to God. For this reason it was commanded in the Old Law that one must not swear except by God.[652] They who swore otherwise violated this order: "By the name of strange gods you shall not

[649] Jer. 4:2.
[650] Wisd. 13:1.
[651] Lev. 24:16.
[652] Deut. 6:13.

swear."[653] Although at times people swear by creatures, nevertheless, it must be known that such is the same as swearing by God. When you swear by your soul or your head, it is as if you bind yourself to be punished by God. Thus: "But I call God to witness upon my soul."[654] And when you swear by the Gospel, you swear by God who gave the Gospel. But they sin who swear either by God or by the Gospel for any trivial reason.

2. To sanctify, we may take God's name justly. Thus, Baptism sanctifies, as St. Paul says: "But you are washed, you are sanctified, and you are justified in the name of our Lord Jesus Christ and the Spirit of God."[655] Baptism, however, does not have power except through the invocation of the Trinity: "But Thou, O Lord, art among us, and Thy name is called upon by us."[656]

3. To expel our adversary, we may take God's name justly. Hence, before Baptism we renounce the Devil: "Only let us be called by Thy name; take away our reproach."[657] Wherefore, if a person returns to his sins, the name of God has been taken in vain.

4. To confess God's name, we may take it justly. "How then shall they call on Him, in whom they have not believed?"[658] And again: "Whosoever shall call upon the name of the Lord shall be saved."[659]

[653] Exod. 23:13.
[654] 2 Cor. 1:23.
[655] 1 Cor. 6:11.
[656] Jer. 14:9.
[657] Isa. 4:1.
[658] Rom. 10:14.
[659] Rom. 10:13.

a. By word of mouth, we confess God's name to show forth the glory of God: "And everyone that calleth upon my name, I have created him for my glory."[660] Accordingly, if a person says anything against the glory of God, he takes the name of God in vain.

b. By our works, we confess God's name when our actions show forth His glory: "That they may see your good works and may glorify your Father who is in Heaven."[661] "Through you the name of God is blasphemed among the Gentiles."[662]

5. To defend ourselves, we take God's name justly. "The name of the Lord is a strong tower; the just runneth to it and shall be exalted."[663] "In my name they shall cast out devils."[664] "There is no other name under Heaven given to men, whereby we must be saved."[665]

6. To make our works complete, we take God's name justly. Thus says the Apostle: "Whatsoever you do in word or work, do it in the name of the Lord Jesus Christ."[666] The reason is because "our help is in the name of the Lord."[667]

Sometimes it happens that a person begins a work imprudently by starting with a vow, for instance, and then does not complete either the work or the vow. And this, again, is taking

---

[660] Isa. 43:7.
[661] Matt. 5:16.
[662] Rom. 2:24.
[663] Prov. 18:10.
[664] Mark 16:17.
[665] Acts 4:12.
[666] Col. 3:17.
[667] Ps. 123:8 (RSV = Ps. 124:8).

God's name in vain. "If thou hast vowed anything to God, defer not to pay it."[668] "Vow and pay to the Lord your God; all ye that are round about Him bring presents."[669] "For an unfaithful and foolish promise displeaseth Him."[670]

---

[668] Eccles. 5:3.
[669] Ps. 75:12 (RSV = Ps. 76:11).
[670] Eccles. 5:3.

III

REMEMBER THAT THOU
KEEP HOLY THE SABBATH DAY

This is the Third Commandment of the Law, and very suitably is it so. For we are first commanded to adore God in our hearts and to worship one God: *Thou shalt not have strange gods before me.* The Second Commandment tells us to revere God in our words: *Thou shalt not take the name of the Lord thy God in vain.* And the Third commands us to revere God in our actions: *Remember that thou keep holy the Sabbath* day.[671] God wished that a certain day be set aside for men to direct their minds to the service of the Lord.

A. Reasons for this commandment

1. **To put aside errors,** we are told to keep holy the Sabbath.

a. The error of those who deny the first creation
The Holy Spirit saw that in the future some men would say that the world had always existed. "In the last days there shall come deceitful scoffers, walking after their own lusts, saying: 'Where is His promise or His coming? For since the time that the fathers slept, all things continue as they were from the beginning of creation.' For of this they are willfully

---

[671] Cf. *Summa Theologica*, I-II, Q. 102, art. 4; II-II, Q. 122, art. 4.

ignorant, that the heavens existed long ago and the earth was formed out of water and through water by the word of God."[672] God, therefore, wished that one day should be set aside in memory of the fact that He created all things in six days and that on the seventh day He rested from the creation of new creatures. This is why the Lord placed this commandment in the Law, saying: *Remember that thou keep holy the Sabbath day.*

b. The error of those who deny the second creation

The Jews kept holy the Sabbath in memory of the first creation, but Christ at His coming brought about a new creation. For by the first creation, an earthly man was created, and by the second, a heavenly man was formed: "For in Christ Jesus neither circumcision availeth anything, nor uncircumcision, but a new creature."[673] This new creation is through grace, which came by the Resurrection: "That as Christ is risen from the dead by the glory of the Father, so we also may walk in newness of life. For if we have been planted together in the likeness of His death, so shall we also be in the likeness of His Resurrection."[674] And thus, because the Resurrection took place on Sunday, we celebrate that day, even as the Jews observed the Sabbath on account of the first creation.

2. To instruct us in our faith in the Redeemer, we are commanded to keep holy the Sabbath. For the flesh of Christ was not corrupted in the sepulcher, and thus it is said: "Moreover my flesh also shall rest in hope."[675] "Nor wilt Thou give Thy

---

[672] 2 Pet. 3:3-5.
[673] Gal. 6:15.
[674] Rom. 6:4-5.
[675] Ps. 15:9 (RSV = Ps. 16:9).

holy one to see corruption."[676] Wherefore God wished that the Sabbath day should be observed and that just as the sacrifices of the Old Law signified the death of Christ, so should the quiet of the Sabbath signify the rest of His body in the sepulcher.

But we do not now observe these sacrifices because with the advent of the reality and the truth, figures of it must cease, just as the darkness is dispelled with the rising of the sun. Nevertheless, we keep the Saturdays in veneration of the Blessed Virgin, in whom remained a firm faith on that Saturday while Christ was dead.

3. To strengthen the promise of rest and to foreshadow its fulfillment, we are commanded to keep holy the Sabbath. For rest indeed was promised to us: "And it shall come to pass on that day, that God shall give thee rest from thy labor, from thy vexation, and from the hard bondage wherewith thou didst serve before."[677] "My people shall sit in the beauty of peace, in the tabernacle of confidence, and in wealthy rest."[678]

We hope for rest from three things: from the labors of the present life, from the struggles of temptations, and from servitude to the Devil. Christ promised this rest to all those who will come to Him: "Come to me, all ye that labor and are burdened, and I will refresh you. Take up my yoke and learn of me, because I am meek and humble of heart; and you shall find rest to your souls. For my yoke is sweet and my burden light."[679]

However, as we know, the Lord worked for six days and on the seventh He rested, because it is necessary in order to do a perfect work: "Behold with your eyes how I have labored a little

[676] Ps. 15:10 (RSV = Ps. 16:10).
[677] Isa. 14:3.
[678] Isa. 32:18.
[679] Matt. 11:28-30.

and have found much rest to myself."[680] For the period of eternity exceeds the present time incomparably more than a thousand years exceeds one day.

4. To increase our love, we are commanded to keep holy the Sabbath. "For the corruptible body is a load upon the soul."[681] And man always tends downward toward earthly things unless he takes means to raise himself above them. It is indeed necessary to have a certain time for this.

In fact, some do this continually: "I will bless the Lord at all times; His praise shall be ever in my mouth."[682] And again: "Pray without ceasing."[683] These shall enjoy the everlasting Sabbath.

There are others who do this (i.e., awaken love for God) during a certain portion of the day: "Seven times a day I have given praise to Thee."[684]

And some, in order to avoid being entirely apart from God, find it necessary to have a fixed day [for worship], lest they become too lukewarm in their love of God: "If you call the Sabbath delightful . . . then shalt thou be delighted in the Lord."[685] Again: "Then shalt thou abound in delights of the Almighty and shalt lift up thy face to God."[686] And accordingly this day is not set aside for the sole exercise of games, but to praise and pray to the Lord God. Wherefore St. Augustine says that it is a lesser evil to plow than to play on this day.[687]

---

[680] Ecclus. 51:35 (RSV = Sir. 51:27).
[681] Wisd. 9:15.
[682] Ps. 33:1 (RSV = Ps. 34:1).
[683] 1 Thess. 5:17.
[684] Ps. 118:164 (RSV = Ps. 119:164).
[685] Isa. 58:13-14.
[686] Job 22:26.
[687] This is a reference to the great public spectacles and games.

5. To exercise works of kindliness to those who are subject to us, we are commanded to keep holy the Sabbath. For some are so cruel to themselves and to others that they labor ceaselessly on account of money. "Observe the day of the Sabbath to sanctify it . . . that thy manservant and thy maidservant may rest, even as thyself."[688]

This commandment, therefore, was given for all of the above reasons.

B. How to keep the Sabbath holy

Remember that you keep holy [sanctify] the Sabbath day. We have already said that as the Jews celebrated the Sabbath, so do we Christians observe Sunday and all principal feasts. Let us now see the way in which we should keep these days.

1. The meanings of *holy*

We ought to know that God did not simply say to "keep" the Sabbath, but to remember to "keep it *holy*." The word *holy* may be taken in two ways:

a. *Holy* signifies "pure"

Sometimes *holy* (or *sanctified*) is the same as "pure," as in: "You are washed; you are sanctified"[689] (i.e., "you are made holy").

b. *Holy* signifies "consecrated"

Then again, at times *holy* is said of a thing consecrated to the worship of God, as, for instance, a place, a season, vestments, and the holy vessels.

---

[688] Deut. 5:12-14.
[689] 1 Cor. 6:11.

191

Therefore, it is in these two ways that we ought to cele-brate the feasts: purely and by giving ourselves over to divine service.

Now, we must consider two things regarding this com-mandment: what we should avoid on a feast day and what we should do.

2. Things to avoid on the Sabbath
We ought to avoid three things. The first is servile work.

a. Servile work

1. Impermissible servile work
"Neither do ye any work; sanctify the Sabbath day."[690] So also it is said in the Law: "You shall do no servile work therein."[691] Now, servile work is bodily work, whereas "free work" (i.e., non-servile work) is done by the mind (for instance, the exercise of the intellect and such like). We also cannot be bound to do this kind of work in a ser-vile manner.

2. Reasons that permit servile work on the Sabbath
We ought to know, however, that servile work can be done on the Sabbath for four reasons:

a. **Necessity.** For this reason, the Lord excused the disciples plucking the ears of corn on the Sabbath, as we read in St. Matthew.[692]

---

[690] Jer. 17:22.
[691] Lev. 23:3.
[692] Matt. 12:3-8.

b. Service of the Church. We see in the same Gospel how the priests did all things necessary in the Temple on the Sabbath day.

c. The good of our neighbor. It was on the Sabbath that the Savior cured one having a withered hand and refuted the Jews who reprimanded Him by citing the example of the sheep in a pit.[693]

d. The authority of our superiors. Thus, God commanded the Jews to circumcise on the Sabbath.[694]

b. Sin

Another thing to be avoided on the Sabbath is sin: "Take heed to your souls and carry no burdens on the Sabbath day."[695] This weight and burden on the soul is sin: "My iniquities as a heavy burden are become heavy upon me."[696] Now, sin is a servile work because "whosoever committeth sin is the servant of sin."[697] Therefore, when it is said, "You shall do no servile work therein," this can be understood of sin. Thus, a person violates this commandment as often as he commits sin on the Sabbath. And so both by working and by sin, God is offended. "Thy Sabbaths and other festivals I will not abide." And why? "Because your assemblies are wicked. My soul hateth your new moons and your solemnities; they are become troublesome to me."[698]

[693] Matt. 12:11-13.
[694] John 7:22-23.
[695] Jer. 17:21.
[696] Ps. 37:5 (RSV = Ps. 38:4).
[697] John 8:34.
[698] Isa. 1:13-14.

c. Idleness

Idleness should also be avoided on the Sabbath: "For idleness hath taught much evil."[699] St. Jerome says: "Be always busy in doing something good, so that the Devil may find you ever occupied."[700] Therefore, it is not good for us to keep only the principal feasts if on the others we remain idle.

"The King's honor loveth judgment" (i.e., discretion).[701] Wherefore we read that certain of the Jews were in hiding and their enemies fell upon them; but they, believing that they were not able to defend themselves on the Sabbath, were overcome and killed.[702] The same thing happens to many who are idle on the feast days: "The enemies have seen her and have mocked at her Sabbaths."[703] But all such should do as those Jews did, of whom it is said: "Whosoever shall come up against us to fight on the Sabbath day, we will fight against him."[704]

3. Things to do on the Sabbath and feast days

Remember that thou keep holy the Sabbath day. We have already said that man must keep the feast days holy and that *holy* is considered in two ways (namely, "pure" and "consecrated to God"). Moreover, we have indicated what things we should abstain from on these days.

Now, it must be shown with what we ought to occupy ourselves.

---

[699] Ecclus. 33:29 (RSV = Sir. 33:27).

[700] *Epistle 125 as Rusticum,* 11.

[701] Ps. 98:4 (RSV = Ps. 99:4).

[702] 1 Macc. 2:31-38.

[703] Lam. 1:7.

[704] 1 Macc. 2:41.

a. Offer sacrifice
In the book of Numbers, God commands that every day one lamb be offered in the morning and one in the evening, but on the Sabbath day the number should be doubled.[705] This shows that on the Sabbath we should offer sacrifice to God from all that we possess: "All things are Thine, and we have given Thee what we received from Thy hand."[706]

1. Our soul as sacrifice
We should offer our soul to God, being sorry for our sins: "A sacrifice to God is an afflicted spirit."[707] And we should pray for His blessings: "Let my prayer be directed as incense in Thy sight."[708] Feast days were instituted for that spiritual joy which is the effect of prayer. Therefore, on such days our prayers should be multiplied.

2. Our body as sacrifice
Second, we should also offer our body by mortifying it with fasting: "Present your bodies as a living sacrifice."[709] And we should praise God: "The sacrifice of praise shall honor me."[710] Therefore, on these days our hymns should be more numerous.

3. Our possessions as sacrifice
Third, we should sacrifice our possessions by giving alms: "And do not forget to do good and to impart, for by such

[705] Num. 28: 3-4, 9.
[706] 1 Paralip. 29:14 (RSV = 1 Chron. 29:14).
[707] Ps. 50:19 (RSV = Ps. 51:17).
[708] Ps. 140:2 (RSV = Ps. 141:2).
[709] Rom. 12:1.
[710] Ps. 49:23 (RSV = Ps. 50:23).

sacrifice God's favor is obtained."[711] These alms ought to be more than on other days, since the Sabbath is a day of common joys: "Send portions to them that have not prepared for themselves, for it is the holy day of the Lord."[712]

b. Hear God's word

Our second duty on the Sabbath is to be eager to hear the word of God. This the Jews did daily: ". . . the voices of the prophets which are read every Sabbath."[713]

Therefore Christians, whose justice should be more perfect, ought to come together on the Sabbath to hear sermons and to participate in the services of the Church: "He that is of God heareth the words of God."[714]

We likewise ought to speak with profit to others: "Let no evil speech proceed from your mouth, but only that speech which is good unto sanctification."[715] These two practices are good for the soul of the sinner because they change his heart for the better: "Are not my words as a fire, saith the Lord, and as a hammer that breaketh the rock in pieces?"[716] The opposite effect is had on those, even the perfect, who neither speak nor hear profitable things: "Evil communications corrupt good manners. Awake, ye just, and sin not."[717] "Thy words have I hidden in my heart."[718] God's

[711] Heb. 13:16.
[712] 2 Esd. 8:10 (RSV = Neh. 8:10).
[713] Acts 13:27.
[714] John 8:47.
[715] Eph. 4:29.
[716] Jer. 23:29.
[717] 1 Cor. 15:33-34.
[718] Ps. 118:11 (RSV = Ps. 119:11).

word enlightens the ignorant: "Thy word is a lamp unto my feet."[719] It inflames the lukewarm: "The word of the Lord inflamed him."[720]

c. Contemplate divine things

The contemplation of divine things may be exercised on the Sabbath. However, this is for the more perfect: "O taste, and see that the Lord is sweet."[721]

1. Rest in divine contemplation

This is for the quiet of the soul, for just as the tired body desires rest, so also does the soul. But the soul's proper rest is in God: "Be Thou unto me a God, a protector, and a house of refuge."[722] "There remaineth therefore a day of rest for the people of God. For he that is entered into his rest, the same also hath rested from his works, as God did from His."[723] "When I go into my house, I shall repose myself with her"[724] (i.e., with Wisdom).

2. Rests that precede divine contemplation

However, before the soul arrives at this rest, three other rests must precede:

a. Rest from the turmoil of sin: "But the wicked are like the raging sea which cannot rest."[725]

---

[719] Ps. 118:105 (RSV = Ps. 119:105).
[720] Ps. 104:19 (RSV = Ps. 105:19).
[721] Ps. 33:9 (RSV = Ps. 34:8).
[722] Ps. 30:3 (RSV = Ps. 31:2).
[723] Heb. 4:9-10.
[724] Wisd. 8:16.
[725] Isa. 57:20.

b. Rest from the passions of the flesh: "For the flesh lusteth against the spirit, and the spirit against the flesh."[726]

c. Rest from the occupations of the world: "Martha, Martha, thou art careful and art troubled about many things."[727]

3. Eternal rest

And then after all these things, the soul rests peacefully in God: "If thou call the Sabbath delightful . . . then shalt thou be delighted in the Lord."[728] The saints gave up everything to possess this rest, "for it is a pearl of great price which a man having found, hid it, and for joy thereof goeth and selleth all that he hath and buyeth that field."[729] This rest in truth is eternal life and heavenly joy: "This is my rest forever and ever; here will I dwell, for I have chosen it."[730]

And to this rest may the Lord bring us all!

[726] Gal. 5:17.
[727] Luke 10:41.
[728] Isa. 58:13-14.
[729] Matt. 13:45-46.
[730] Ps. 131:14 (RSV = Ps. 132:14).

HONOR THY FATHER AND THY MOTHER, THAT THOU MAYEST BE LONG-LIVED UPON THE LAND WHICH THE LORD THY GOD WILL GIVE THEE

Perfection for man consists in the love of God and of neighbor. The three commandments on the first tablet pertain to the love of God; the seven on the second pertain to the love of neighbor.

We must "love, not in word nor in tongue, but in deed and in truth."[731] For a man to love thus, he must avoid evil and do good. Thus, some of the Commandments prescribe good acts, and others forbid evil deeds. Also, although avoiding evil is within our power, we are incapable of doing good to everyone. Thus, St. Augustine says that we should love all, but we are not bound to do good to all.

A. Reasons we should honor our parents

1. Their union with us

Among those to whom we are bound to do good are those in some way united to us. Thus, "If any man have not care of his own and especially of those of his house, he hath denied the Faith."[732] Now, among all our relatives, there are none closer

[731] 1 John 3:18.
[732] 1 Tim. 5:8.

than our father and mother. "We ought to love God first," says St. Ambrose, "then our father and mother." Hence, God has given us the commandment: *Honor thy father and thy mother*.[733]

2. The benefits they have given us

The Philosopher also gives another reason for this honor to parents, in that we cannot make an equal return to our parents for the great benefits they have granted us. Therefore, an offended parent has the right to send his son away, but the son has no such right.[734] Parents, indeed, provide three benefits to children:

a. Being

The first is that they bring us into being: "Honor thy father, and forget not the groanings of thy mother; remember that thou hadst not been born but through them."[735]

b. Nourishment and support

Second, they furnish us nourishment and the support necessary for life. For a child comes naked into the world, as Job relates,[736] but his parents provide for him.

c. Instruction

Instruction is the third benefit that parents provide children: "We have had fathers of our flesh for instructors."[737] "Hast thou children? Instruct them."[738] Parents, therefore, should give instruction without delay to their children because "a

---

[733] Cf. *Summa Theologica*, II-II, Q. 122, art. 5; Q. 101, art. 2, 4.

[734] Aristotle, *Nichomachean Ethics*, 1163b.

[735] Ecclus. 7:29-30 (RSV = Ps. 7:27-28).

[736] Job 1:21.

[737] Heb. 12:9.

[738] Ecclus. 7:25 (RSV = Sir. 7:23).

young man according to his way, even when he is old, will not depart from it."[739] And again: "It is good for a man when he hath borne the yoke from his youth."[740] Now, the instruction which Tobias gave his son was this: to fear the Lord and to abstain from sin.[741] This is indeed contrary to those parents who approve of the misdeeds of their children.

Children therefore receive from their parents birth, nourishment, and instruction.

B. Obligations to parents that arise from these benefits
In return for these benefits, we owe our parents three things:

1. Honor, because they gave us existence
Since we owe our birth to our parents, we ought to honor them more than any other superiors, because from those others we receive only temporal things: "He that feareth the Lord honoreth his parents and will serve them as his masters that brought him into the world. Honor thy father in work and word and all patience, that a blessing may come upon thee from him."[742] In doing this, you shall also honor yourself, because "the glory of a man is from honor of his father, and a father without honor is the disgrace of his son."[743]

2. Support, because they gave us nourishment
Since we receive nourishment from our parents in our childhood, we must support them in their old age: "Son, support the

[739] Prov. 22:6.
[740] Lam. 3:27.
[741] Tob. 4:5.
[742] Ecclus. 3:8-10 (RSV = Sir. 3:6-8).
[743] Ecclus. 3:13 (RSV = Sir. 3:11).

old age of thy father, and grieve him not in his life. And if his understanding fail, have patience with him and despise him not when thou art in thy strength. . . . Of what an evil fame is he that forsaketh his father! And he is cursed of God that angereth his mother."[744]

For the humiliation of those who act contrary to this, Cassiodorus relates how young storks (when their parents have lost their feathers because of approaching old age and are unable to find suitable food) make the parent storks comfortable with their own feathers and bring back food for their worn-out bodies. Thus, by this affectionate exchange, the young ones repay the parents for what they received when they were young.[745]

3. Obedience, because they gave us instruction

We must obey our parents, for they have instructed us. "Children, obey your parents in all things."[746] This excepts, of course, those things which are contrary to God. St. Jerome says that the only loyalty in such cases is to be cruel.[747] "If any man hate not his father and mother . . . he cannot be my disciple."[748] This is to say that God is in the truest sense our Father: "Is not He thy Father who hath possessed thee, made thee, and created thee?"[749]

C. Rewards for honoring our parents

Honor thy father and thy mother. Among all the Commandments, this one only has the additional words: *that thou mayest be long-lived upon the land.* The reason for this is lest it be thought that there is

---

[744] Ecclus. 3:14-15, 18 (RSV = Sir. 3:12-13, 16).

[745] *Variarum*, Lib. 2, Ep. 14.

[746] Col. 3:20.

[747] *Epistle 14 ad Heliodorum*, 2-3.

[748] Luke 14:26.

[749] Deut. 32:6.

no reward for those who honor their parents, seeing that it is a natural obligation. Hence it must be known that five most desirable rewards are promised to those who honor their parents.

1. Grace and glory

The first reward is grace for the present life and glory in the life to come, which surely are greatly to be desired: "Honor thy father . . . that a blessing may come upon thee from him and his blessing may remain in the end."[750]

The very opposite comes upon those who dishonor their parents. Indeed, they are cursed in the Law by God.[751] It is also written: "He that is unjust in that which is little is unjust also in that which is greater."[752]

But this our natural life is as nothing compared with the life of grace. And so, therefore, if you do not acknowledge the blessing of the natural life which you owe to your parents, then you are unworthy of the life of grace, which is greater, and all the more unworthy of the life of glory, which is the greatest of all blessings.

2. A long life

The second reward is a long life: *that thou mayest be long-lived upon the land*. For "he that honoreth his father shall enjoy a long life."[753] Now, this means a long life which is a full life; and it is not observed in time but in activity, as the Philosopher observes. Life, however, is full inasmuch as it is a life of virtue. So a man who is virtuous and holy enjoys a long life even if in body he dies young: "Being perfect in a short space, he fulfilled a long

[750] Ecclus. 3:9-10 (RSV = Sir. 3:8-9).
[751] Deut. 27:16.
[752] Luke 16:10.
[753] Ecclus. 3:7 (RSV = Sir. 3:6).

time — for his soul pleased God."[754] Thus, for example, he is a good merchant who does as much business in one day as another would do in a year. And note well that it sometimes happens that a temporally long life may lead up to a spiritual as well as a bodily death, as was the case with Judas.

The reward for keeping this commandment is a long life for the body. The very opposite (death) is the fate of those who dishonor their parents. We receive our life from them; and just as soldiers owe fealty to the king and lose their rights in case of any treachery, so also they who dishonor their parents deserve to forfeit their lives: "The eye that mocketh at his father and that despiseth the labor of his mother in bearing him, let the ravens pick it out and the young eagles eat it."[755] Here the *ravens* signify officials of kings and princes, who in turn are the *young eagles*.

But if it happens that such are not bodily punished, they nevertheless cannot escape the death of the soul. It is not well, therefore, for a father to give too much power to his children: "Give not to son or wife, brother or friend, power over thee while thou livest; and give not thy estate to another, lest thou repent."[756]

3. Grateful and pleasing children

The third reward is to have in turn grateful and pleasing children. For a father naturally treasures his children, but the contrary is not always the case: "He that honoreth his father shall have joy in his own children."[757] Again: "With what measure you measure, it shall be measured to you again."[758]

---

[754] Wisd. 4:13-14.
[755] Prov. 30:17.
[756] Ecclus. 33:20 (RSV = Sir. 33:19).
[757] Ecclus. 3:6 (RSV = Sir. 3:5).
[758] Matt. 7:2.

4. A praiseworthy reputation

The fourth reward is a praiseworthy reputation: "For the glory of a man is from the honor of his father."[759] And again: "Of what an evil fame is he that forsaketh his father."[760]

5. Riches

A fifth reward is riches: "The father's blessing establisheth the houses of his children, but the mother's curse rooteth up the foundation."[761]

D. Others who deserve the reverence due to fathers

Honor thy father and thy mother. A man is called *father* not only by reason of generation but also for other reasons, and to each of these there is due a certain reverence.

1. The Apostles and saints are called *fathers* because of their doctrine and their exemplification of faith: "Although you have ten thousand instructors in Christ, yet you have not many fathers. For in Christ Jesus, by the gospel, I have begotten you."[762] And again: "Let us now praise men of renown and our fathers in their generation."[763] However, let us praise them not in word only but by imitating them. And we do this if nothing is found in us contrary to what we praise in them.

2. Our superiors in the Church are also called *fathers*. They, too, are to be respected as the ministers of God: "Remember your prelates. . . . Consider the outcome of their life and imitate

---

[759] Ecclus. 3:13 (RSV = Sir. 3:11).
[760] Ecclus. 3:18 (RSV = Sir. 3:16).
[761] Ecclus. 3:11 (RSV = Sir. 3:9).
[762] 1 Cor. 4:15.
[763] Ecclus. 44:1 (RSV = Sir. 44:1).

their faith."[764] And again: "He that heareth you, heareth me; and he that despiseth you, despiseth me."[765] We honor our prelates by showing them obedience ("Obey your prelates, and be subject to them"[766]) and also by paying them tithes ("Honor the Lord with thy substance and give Him of the first of thy fruits").[767]

3. Rulers and kings are called *fathers:* "Father, if the prophet had bid thee do some great thing, surely thou shouldst have done it."[768] We call them *fathers* because their whole care is the good of their people. And we honor them by being subject to them: "Let every soul be subject to the governing authorities."[769] We should be subject to them not merely through fear, but through love; and not merely because it is reasonable, but because of the dictates of our conscience, because "there is no authority but from God."[770] And so to all such must we render what is due to them: "Tribute, to whom tribute is due; custom, to whom custom; fear, to whom fear; and honor, to whom honor."[771] And again: "My son, fear the Lord and the king."[772]

4. Our benefactors are also called *fathers:* "Be merciful to the fatherless as a father."[773] He, too, [who gives his bond] is like a father, of whom it is said: "Forget not the kindness of thy

[764] Heb. 13:7.
[765] Luke 10:16.
[766] Heb. 13:17.
[767] Prov. 3:9.
[768] 4 Kings 5:13 (RSV = 2 Kings 5:13).
[769] Rom. 13:1.
[770] Ibid.
[771] Rom. 13:7.
[772] Prov. 24:21.
[773] Ecclus. 4:10 (RSV = Sir. 4:10).

surety."[774] On the other hand, the ungrateful shall receive a punishment such as is written: "The hope of the ungrateful shall melt away as the winter's ice."[775]

5. Old men also are called *fathers*: "Ask thy father and he will declare to thee; thy elders and they will tell thee."[776] And again: "Rise up before the hoary head and honor the person of the aged man."[777] "In the company of great men take not upon thee to speak; and when the ancients are present, speak not much."[778] "Hear in silence, and for thy reverence good grace shall come to thee."[779]

Now, all these fathers must be honored because they all resemble to some degree our Father who is in Heaven. And of all of them it is said: "He that despiseth you, despiseth me."

---

[774] Ecclus. 29:19 (RSV = Sir. 29:15).
[775] Wisd. 16:29.
[776] Deut. 32:7.
[777] Lev. 19:32.
[778] Ecclus. 32:13 (RSV = Sir. 32:9).
[779] Ecclus. 32:9 (No equivalent in RSV).

V

THOU SHALT NOT KILL

In the divine law, which tells us that we must love God and our
neighbor, it is commanded that we not only do good but also avoid
evil. The greatest evil that can be done to one's neighbor is to take
his life. This is prohibited in the commandment: *Thou shalt not
kill.*[780]

A. Killing

1. Errors regarding killing

In connection with this commandment there are errors regarding the killing of animals, the execution of criminals, and
suicide.

a. The killing of animals

Some have said that it is not permitted to kill even brute animals. But this is false, because it is not a sin to use that
which is subordinate to the power of man. It is in the natural order that plants nourish animals, certain animals nourish others, and all nourish man: "Even as the green herbs
have I delivered them all to you."[781] The Philosopher says

---

[780] Cf. *Summa Theologica*, II-II, Q. 69, art. 2, 3; Q. 112, art. 6.
[781] Gen. 9:3.

that hunting is like a just war.[782] And St. Paul says: "Whatsoever is sold in the meat market eat, asking no questions for conscience' sake."[783] Therefore, the sense of the commandment is: "Thou shalt not kill *men.*"

b. The execution of criminals

Some have held that the killing of man is prohibited altogether. They believe that judges in the civil courts are murderers when they condemn men to death according to the laws.

Against this St. Augustine says that God by this commandment does not take away from Himself the right to kill. Thus, we read: "I will kill, and I will make to live."[784] It is, therefore, lawful for a judge to kill according to a mandate from God, since in this act God operates and every law is a command of God: "By me kings reign and lawgivers decree just things."[785] And again: "For if thou dost that which is evil, fear; for he beareth not the sword in vain, because he is God's minister. . . ."[786] To Moses also was it said: "Wizards thou shalt not suffer to live."[787] Thus that which is lawful to God is lawful for His ministers when they act by His mandate.

It is evident that God, who is the author of laws, has every right to inflict death on account of sin. For "the wages of sin is death."[788] Neither does His minister sin in inflicting

---

[782] Aristotle, *Politics*, 1256b.
[783] 1 Cor. 10:25.
[784] Deut. 32:39.
[785] Prov. 8:15.
[786] Rom. 13:4.
[787] Exod. 22:18.
[788] Rom. 6:23.

THOU SHALT NOT KILL

that punishment. The sense, therefore, of *Thou shalt not kill*
is that one shall not kill by one's own authority.

c. Suicide

There are those who held that although this commandment
forbids a person to kill another person, yet it is lawful to kill
oneself. Thus, there are the examples of Samson[789] and Cato
and certain virgins who threw themselves into the flames, as
St. Augustine relates in *The City of God*.[790] But he also explains this in the words: "He who kills himself certainly kills
a man."[791]

If it is not lawful to kill except by the authority of God,
then it is not lawful to kill oneself except either upon the authority of God or as instructed by the Holy Spirit, as was the
case of Samson. Therefore: *Thou shalt not kill.*

2. Ways of killing a man's body

One may kill a man in several ways.

a. By one's own hand: "Your hands are full of blood."[792] This
is not only against charity, which tells us to love our neighbor as ourself: "No murderer hath eternal life abiding in
himself."[793] But it is also against nature, for "every beast
loveth its like."[794] And so it is said: "He that striketh a man
with a will to kill him shall be put to death."[795] He who does

---

[789] Judg. 16:28-30.
[790] *The City of God*, Bk. 1, ch. 27.
[791] Ibid.
[792] Isa. 1:15.
[793] 1 John 3:15.
[794] Ecclus. 13:19 (RSV = Sir. 13:15).
[795] Exod. 21:12.

this is more cruel than the wolf, of which Aristotle says that one wolf will not eat of the flesh of another wolf.[796]

b. By word of mouth, we can kill, by giving counsel to anyone against another by provocation, accusation, or detraction: ". . . the sons of men whose teeth are weapons and arrows, and their tongue a sharp sword."[797]

c. By helping another kill, we can kill, as it is written: "My son, walk not thou with them . . . for their feet run to evil, and they make haste to shed blood."[798]

d. By consenting to another's death, we can kill: "They who do such things are worthy of death; and not only they that do them, but also they that consent to them that do them."[799]

e. By not preventing another's death, we can kill: "Deliver them that are led to death."[800] If we can prevent it, yet, through negligence or avarice, do not do so, we also kill. Thus, St. Ambrose says: "Give food to him that is dying of hunger; if you do not, you are his murderer."

3. Ways of killing a man's soul

We have already considered the killing of the body, but some also kill the soul by drawing it away from the life of grace, specifically by inducing it to commit mortal sin: "He was a

---

[796] *De Historia Animalium*, 571b.
[797] Ps. 56:5 (RSV = Ps. 57:4).
[798] Prov. 1:15-16.
[799] Rom. 1:32.
[800] Prov. 24:11.

murderer from the beginning"[801] (i.e., insofar as he drew men into sin).

4. Ways of killing both body and soul
Others, however, slay both body and soul, and in two ways:

a. By the murder of one with child, whereby the child is killed both in body and soul.

b. By committing suicide

B. Anger
In the Gospel of St. Matthew[802] Christ taught that our justice should be greater than the justice of the Old Law. This means that Christians should observe the Commandments of the Law more perfectly than the Jews observed them.

The reason is that greater effort deserves a better reward: "He who soweth sparingly shall also reap sparingly."[803] The Old Law promised a temporary and earthly reward: "If you be willing and will hearken to me, you shall eat the good things of the land."[804] But in the New Law heavenly and eternal things are promised. Therefore, justice, which is the observance of the Commandments, should be more generous among Christians, because they expect a greater reward.

1. Anger and killing
The Lord specifically mentioned this commandment when He said: "You have heard that it was said to them of old: *Thou shalt*

[801] John 8:44.
[802] Matt. 5:17-48.
[803] 2 Cor. 9:6.
[804] Isa. 1:19.

213

not kill. . . . But I say to you that anyone who is angry with his brother shall be in danger of the judgment."[805] By this is meant the penalty which the Law prescribes: "If a man kill his neighbor on set purpose and by lying in wait for him . . . take him away from my altar, that he may die."[806]

2. Obligations regarding anger

a. Be not quickly provoked to anger
"Let men be swift to hear, but slow to speak and slow to anger."[807] There are two reasons for this.

1. Anger is virtuous only sometimes

a. The wise man is properly subject to moderate anger
Anger is a sin punished by God, but is all anger contrary to virtue? There are two opinions about this. The Stoics said that the wise man is free from all passions. Even more, they maintained that true virtue consists in perfect quiet of soul. The Peripatetics, on the other hand, held that the wise man is subject to anger but in a moderate degree. This is the more accurate opinion.

1. Christ was angry sometimes
It is first proven by authority, for the Gospel shows that these passions were attributed to Christ, in whom was the full fountainhead of wisdom.

---

[805] Matt. 5:21-22.
[806] Exod. 21:14.
[807] James 1:19.

THOU SHALT NOT KILL

2. Anger sometimes has a good purpose

Second, it is proven from reason. If all the passions were opposed to virtue, then there would be some powers of the soul which would be without good purpose. Indeed, they would be positively harmful to man, since they would have no acts in keeping with them. Thus, the irascible and concupiscible powers would be given to man to no purpose.

It must therefore be concluded that sometimes anger is virtuous and sometimes it is not.

b. The kinds of anger

We see this if we consider anger in three different ways.

1. Anger can be a judgment of reason

First, we find anger as it exists solely in the judgment of reason, without any perturbation of soul. This is more properly not anger but judgment. Thus, the Lord punishing the wicked is said to be angry: "I will bear the wrath of the Lord because I have sinned against Him."[808]

2. Righteous anger

Anger is considered a passion. This is in the sensitive appetite and is twofold. Sometimes it is ordered by reason or restrained within proper limits by reason, as when a person is angry because it is justly fitting to be angry and within proper limits. This is an act of virtue and is called *righteous anger*.

[808] Mic. 7:9.

Thus, the Philosopher says that meekness is not opposed to anger. This kind of anger, then, is not a sin.

3. Sinful anger

Anger which overthrows the judgment of reason is always sinful, sometimes mortally and sometimes venially. And whether it is one or the other will depend on that object to which the anger incites, which is sometimes mortal, sometimes venial.

a. Mortally sinful anger

Sin may be mortal in two ways: either in its *genus* or by reason of its circumstances. For example, murder would seem to be a mortal sin in its genus because it is directly opposite to a divine commandment.

Thus, consent to murder is a mortal sin in its *genus* because if an act itself is a mortal sin, then consent to the act will be a mortal sin as well.

b. Venially sinful anger

Sometimes, however, an act itself is mortal in its *genus* but, nevertheless, the impulse is not mortal because it is without consent. This is the same as when one is moved by the impulse of concupiscence to fornication and yet does not consent: here one does not commit a sin.

The same holds true of anger. For anger is really the impulse to avenge an injury which one has suffered. Now, if this impulse of the passion is so great that reason is weakened, then it is a mortal sin.

On the other hand, if, up to the moment of consent, the reason is not perverted by the passion (and if consent is given without any perversion of the reason), then there is no mortal sin. "Whosoever is angry with his brother shall be in danger of the judgment."[809] This must be understood of that impulse of passion tending to do injury to the extent that reason is perverted. This impulse, inasmuch as it is consented to, is a mortal sin.

2. Anger diminishes freedom
The second reason we should not be easily provoked to anger is that every man loves liberty and hates restraint. But he who is filled with anger is not master of himself: "Who can bear the violence of one provoked?"[810] And again: "A stone is heavy and sand weighty, but the anger of a fool is heavier than both."[811]

b. Do not remain angry long
We should also take care that we do not remain angry very long: "Be ye angry and sin not."[812] And: "Let not the sun go down upon your anger."[813] The reason for this is given in the Gospel by our Lord: "Be at agreement with thy adversary betimes whilst thou art in the way with him, lest perhaps thy

[809] Matt. 5:21.
[810] Prov. 27:4.
[811] Prov. 27:3.
[812] Ps. 4:5 (RSV = Ps. 4:4).
[813] Eph. 4:26.

adversary deliver thee to the judge, the judge deliver thee to the officer, and thou be cast into prison. Amen, I say unto thee, thou shalt not go out from hence till thou repay the last farthing."[814]

c. Control the intensity of your anger
We should beware lest our anger grow in intensity, having its beginning in the heart and finally leading on to hatred. For there is this difference between anger and hatred, that anger is sudden but hatred is long-lived and, thus, is a mortal sin: "Whosoever hateth his brother is a murderer."[815] And the reason is that he kills both himself (by destroying charity) and another. Thus, St. Augustine in his *Rule* says: "Let there be no quarrels among you; or if they do arise, then let them end quickly, lest anger should grow into hatred, the mote become a beam, and the soul become a murderer."[816] Again: "A passionate man stirreth up strifes."[817] "Cursed be their fury because it was stubborn, and their wrath because it was cruel."[818]

d. Do not let wrath explode in angry words
We must take care lest our wrath explode in angry words: "A fool immediately showeth his anger."[819] Now, angry words are twofold in effect: either they injure another or they express one's own pride in oneself. Our Lord referred to the first when He said, "And whosoever shall say to his brother,

[814] Matt. 5:25-26.
[815] 1 John 3:15.
[816] *Epistle*, 211, 14.
[817] Prov. 15:18.
[818] Gen. 49:7.
[819] Prov. 12:16.

'Thou fool,' shall be in danger of hellfire."[820] And He referred to the latter in the words: "And he that shall say, 'Raca,' shall be in danger of the council."[821] Moreover: "A mild answer breaketh wrath, but a harsh word stirreth up fury."[822]

e. Do not let anger lead to evil deeds

Finally, we must beware lest anger provoke us to deeds. In all our dealings we should observe two things: justice and mercy. But anger hinders us in both: "For the anger of a man worketh not the justice of God."[823] Such a one may indeed be willing, but his anger prevents him. A certain philosopher once said to a man who had offended him: "I would punish you, were I not angry." "Anger hath no mercy, nor fury when it breaketh forth."[824] "In their fury they slew a man."[825]

It is for all this that Christ taught us to beware not only of murder but also of anger. The good physician removes the external symptoms of a malady. Furthermore, he even removes the very root of the illness so that there will be no relapse. So, also, the Lord wishes us to avoid the beginnings of sins. Thus, anger should be avoided because it is the beginning of murder.

[820] Matt. 5:22.
[821] Ibid.
[822] Prov. 15:1.
[823] James 1:20.
[824] Prov. 27:4.
[825] Gen. 49:6.

VI

THOU SHALT NOT COMMIT ADULTERY

A. Adultery

After the prohibition of murder, adultery is forbidden. This is fitting, since husband and wife are as one body. "They shall be," says the Lord, "two in one flesh."[826] Therefore, after an injury inflicted upon a man in his own person, none is so grave as that which is inflicted upon a person with whom he is joined.[827] Adultery is forbidden both to the wife and the husband.

1. Adultery of the wife

We shall consider first the adultery of the wife, since in this seems to lie the greater sin. For a wife who commits adultery is guilty of three grave sins which are implied in the following words: "So every woman that leaveth her husband, . . . first, she hath been unfaithful to the Law of the Most High; second, she hath offended against her husband; and third, she hath fornicated in adultery and hath gotten her children of another man."[828]

a. Infidelity to the Law of God

First, therefore, the adulteress has sinned by lack of faith, for she is unfaithful to the Law wherein God has forbidden

---

[826] Gen. 2:24.
[827] Cf. *Summa Theologica*, II-II, Q. 122, art. 6; Q. 154.
[828] Ecclus. 23:32-33 (RSV = Sir. 23:22-23).

221

adultery. Moreover, she has spurned the ordinance of God: "What therefore God has joined together, let no man put asunder."[829]

Also she has sinned against the institution or sacrament, because marriage is contracted before the eyes of the Church and thereupon God is called, as it were, to witness a bond of fidelity which must be kept: "The Lord hath been witness between thee and the wife of thy youth whom thou hast despised."[830] Therefore, she has sinned against the Law of God, against a precept of the Church, and against a sacrament of God.

b. Infidelity to her husband

Second, the adulteress sins by infidelity, because she has betrayed her husband: "The wife hath not power of her own body, but the husband."[831] In fact, without the consent of the husband, she cannot observe celibacy. If adultery is committed, then, an act of treachery is perpetrated in that the wife gives herself to another, just as if a servant gave himself to another master: "She forsaketh the guide of her youth and hath forgotten the covenant of her God."[832]

c. Theft

Third, the adulteress commits the sin of theft in that she brings forth children from a man who is not her husband. This is a most grave theft in that she expends her heredity upon children who are not her husband's. Let it be noted that such a one should encourage her children to enter

---

[829] Matt. 19:6.
[830] Mal. 2:14.
[831] 1 Cor. 7:4.
[832] Prov. 2:17-18.

religion or upon such a walk of life that they do not succeed in the property of her husband.

Therefore, an adulteress is guilty of sacrilege, treachery, and theft.

2. Adultery of the husband

Husbands, however, do not sin any less than wives, although they sometimes may salve themselves to the contrary. This is clear for three reasons.

a. Violation of the equality of rights between spouses

First, adultery is a sin because it violates the equality which holds between husband and wife, for "the husband also hath not power of his own body, but the wife."[833] Therefore, as far as the rights of Matrimony are concerned, one cannot act without the consent of the other. As an indication of this, God did not form woman from the foot or from the head, but from the rib of the man. Now, marriage was at no time a perfect state until the law of Christ came, because a Jewish husband could have many wives, but a Jewish wife could not have many husbands. Hence, equality did not exist.

b. Defect of strength

Second, adultery is a sin because strength is a special quality of the man, while the passion proper to the woman is concupiscence: "Ye husbands, likewise dwelling with them according to knowledge, giving honor to the female as to the weaker vessel."[834] Therefore, if you ask from your wife what you do not keep yourself, then you are unfaithful.

[833] 1 Cor. 7:4.
[834] 1 Pet. 3:7.

c. Undermining the authority of the husband

Third, adultery is a sin because of the authority of the husband. For the husband is head of the wife and, as is said, "Women may not speak in the church. . . . If they would learn anything, let them ask their husbands at home."[835] The husband is the teacher of his wife. God, therefore, gave the commandment to the husband.

Now, as regards fulfillment of their duties, a priest who fails is more guilty than a layman and a bishop more than a priest, because it is especially incumbent upon them to teach others. In like manner, the husband who commits adultery breaks faith by not obeying that which he ought. Thus, God forbids adultery both to men and women.

B. Fornication and impurity

Now, it must be known that although some believe that adultery is a sin, yet they do not believe that simple fornication is a mortal sin. Against them stand the words of St. Paul: "For fornicators and adulterers God will judge."[836] "Do not err: neither fornicators . . . nor adulterers, nor the effeminate, nor those who lie shall possess the kingdom of God."[837] Since only mortal sin excludes us from the kingdom of God, fornication must be a mortal sin.

But one might say that there is no reason why fornication should be a mortal sin, since the body of the wife is not given, as in adultery. I say, however, if the body of the wife is not given, nevertheless, there is given the body of Christ which was given to the husband when he was sanctified in Baptism.

If, then, a husband must not betray his wife, with much more reason must he not be unfaithful to Christ: "Know you not that

---

[835] 1 Cor. 14:34-35.
[836] Heb. 13:4.
[837] 1 Cor. 6:9.

your bodies are the members of Christ? Shall I then take the members of Christ and make them the members of a harlot? God forbid!"[838] It is heretical to say that fornication is not a mortal sin.

Moreover, it must be known that this commandment does not merely forbid adultery but also every form of immodesty and impurity.

C. Married intercourse

There are some who say that intercourse between married persons is not devoid of sin. But this is heretical, for the Apostle says: "Let marriage be honorable in all and the bed undefiled."[839] Not only is it devoid of sin but, for those in the state of grace, it is meritorious for eternal life. Sometimes, however, it may be a venial sin and sometimes a mortal sin.

1. For procreation: When it is had with the intention of bringing forth offspring, married intercourse is an act of virtue.

2. For mutual comfort: When it is had with the intent of rendering mutual comfort, married intercourse is an act of justice.

3. For the excitement of lust: When it is a cause of exciting lust, although within the limits of marriage, married intercourse is a venial sin.

4. For illicit ends: When married intercourse goes beyond these limits so as to intend intercourse with another, if possible, it is a mortal sin.

[838] 1 Cor. 6:15.
[839] Heb. 13:4.

D. The prohibition of adultery and fornication

Adultery and fornication are forbidden for a number of reasons.

1. They destroy the soul

First, adultery and fornication are forbidden because they destroy the soul: "He that is an adulterer shall destroy his own soul through the folly of his heart."[840] It says *through the folly of his heart*, which means "whenever the flesh dominates the spirit."

2. They destroy life

Second, adultery and fornication deprive one of life, for one guilty of such should die according to the Law, as we read in Leviticus[841] and Deuteronomy.[842] Sometimes the guilty one is not punished bodily in this life, which is to his disadvantage, since punishment of the body may be borne with patience and is conducive to the remission of sins. Nevertheless, he shall be punished in the future life.

3. They waste substance

Third, adultery and fornication consume a person's substance, just as happened to the prodigal son in that "he wasted his substance living riotously."[843] "Give not thy soul to harlots in any way, lest thou destroy thyself and thy inheritance."[844]

4. They defile offspring

Fourth, adultery and fornication defile offspring: "The children of adulterers shall not come to perfection, and the seed of the

---

[840] Prov. 6:32.
[841] Lev. 20:10.
[842] Deut. 22:22.
[843] Luke 15:13.
[844] Ecclus. 9:6 (RSV = Sir. 9:6).

unlawful bed shall be rooted out. And if they live long, they shall be nothing regarded and their last old age shall be without honor."[845] And again: "Otherwise your children should be unclean, but now they are holy."[846] Thus, they are never honored in the Church, but if they be clerics their dishonor may go without shame.

5. They destroy honor

Fifth, adultery and fornication take away one's honor and this especially is applicable to women: "Every woman that is a harlot shall be trodden upon as dung in the way."[847] And of the husband it is said: "He gathereth to himself shame and dishonor, and his reproach shall not be blotted out."[848]

St. Gregory says that sins of the flesh are more shameful and less blameful than those of the spirit, and the reason is because they are common to the beasts. "Man when he was in honor did not understand; and he hath been compared to senseless beasts, and made like to them."[849]

---

[845] Wisd. 3:16-17.

[846] 1 Cor. 7:14.

[847] Ecclus. 9:10 (No equivalent in RSV).

[848] Prov. 6:33.

[849] Ps. 48:21 (RSV = Ps. 49:20).

VII

THOU SHALT NOT STEAL

In the Commandments, the Lord specifically forbids injury to our neighbor. Thus, *Thou shalt not kill* forbids us to injure our neighbor in his own person; *Thou shalt not commit adultery* forbids injury to the person to whom one is bound in marriage; and now *Thou shalt not steal* forbids us to injure our neighbor in his goods. This commandment forbids us to take wrongfully any worldly goods whatsoever.[850]

A. Ways of stealing
Theft can be committed in a number of ways:

1. By taking stealthily, theft can be committed: "If the householder had known the hour that the thief would come. . . ."[851] Stealing is an act wholly blameworthy because it is a form of treachery. "Shame . . . is upon the thief."[852]

2. By taking with violence, theft can likewise be committed. This is even a greater injury: "They have violently robbed the fatherless."[853] Among those who do such things are wicked

---

[850] Cf. *Summa Theologica*, II-II, Q. 122, art. 6.
[851] Matt. 24:43.
[852] Ecclus. 5:17 (RSV = Sir. 5:14).
[853] Job 24:9.

kings and rulers: "Her princes are in the midst of her as roaring lions; her judges are evening wolves who have left nothing for the morning."[854] They act contrary to the will of God, who wishes a rule according to justice: "By me kings reign and lawgivers decree just things."[855] Sometimes they do such things stealthily and sometimes with violence: "Thy princes are faithless companions of thieves. They all love bribes; they run after rewards."[856] At times they steal by enacting laws and enforcing them for profit only: "Woe to them that make wicked laws."[857] And St. Augustine says that every wrongful usurpation is theft when he asks: "What are thrones but forms of thievery?"[858]

3. By not paying wages that are due, theft can be committed: "The wages of him that hath been hired by thee shall not abide by thee until the morning."[859] This means that a man must pay everyone his due, whether he be prince, prelate, or cleric: "Render therefore to all men their dues: tribute, to whom tribute is due; custom, to whom custom."[860] Hence, we are bound to give a return to rulers who guard our safety.

4. By fraudulent buying and selling, theft can be committed: "Thou shalt not have diverse weights in thy bag, a greater and a lesser."[861] And again: "Do not any unjust thing in judgment, in

---

[854] Soph. 3:3 (RSV: Zeph. 3:3).
[855] Prov. 8:15.
[856] Isa. 1:23.
[857] Isa. 10:1.
[858] *The City of God,* Bk. 4, ch. 4.
[859] Lev. 19:13.
[860] Rom. 13:7.
[861] Deut. 25:13.

rule, in weight, or in measure."[862] All this is directed against the keepers of wineshops who mix water with the wine. Usury is also forbidden: "Who shall dwell in Thy tabernacle, or who shall rest in Thy holy hill? . . . He that hath not put his money out to usury."[863] This is also directed against moneychangers who commit many frauds and against the sellers of cloth and other goods.

5. **By buying promotions** to positions of temporal or spiritual honor, theft can be committed. "The riches which he hath swallowed, he shall vomit up; and God shall draw them out of his belly"[864] has reference to temporal position. Thus, all tyrants who hold by force a kingdom, province, or land are thieves and are held to restitution. Concerning spiritual dignities it is said: "Amen, amen, I say to you, he that entereth not by the door into the sheepfold but climbeth up another way is a thief and a robber."[865] Therefore, they who commit simony are thieves.

B. Reasons stealing is forbidden

Thou shalt not steal. This commandment, as has been said, forbids taking things wrongfully. We can bring forth many reasons why it is given.

1. The gravity of the sin

The first is because of the gravity of this sin, which is likened to murder: "The bread of the needy is the life of the poor; he that defraudeth them thereof is a man of blood."[866] And again: "He

---

[862] Lev. 19:35-36.
[863] Ps. 14:1, 5 (RSV = Ps. 15:1, 5).
[864] Job 20:15.
[865] John 10:1.
[866] Ecclus. 34:25 (RSV = Sir. 34:21).

that sheddeth blood and he that defraudeth the laborer of his hire are brothers."[867]

2. The unique dangers of theft

Stealing is forbidden because of the peculiar danger involved in theft: no sin is so dangerous. After committing other sins a person may quickly repent. For instance, a person can repent of murder when his anger cools or of fornication when his passion subsides. But even after he repents of stealing, it is still hard to make the necessary satisfaction by fulfilling the obligation of restitution and the duty to make up for the loss incurred by the rightful owner.

These duties are above and beyond the obligation to repent of the sin itself: "Woe to him that heapeth together that which is not his own! How long doth he load himself with thick clay?"[868] For a person cannot easily extricate himself from thick clay.

3. The uselessness of stolen goods

Stealing is also forbidden because of the uselessness of stolen goods, for they are of no spiritual value: "Treasures of wickedness shall profit nothing."[869] Wealth can indeed be useful for almsgiving and offering of sacrifices, for "the ransom of a man's life are his riches."[870] But it is said of stolen goods: "I am the Lord who loves judgment and hates robbery in a holocaust."[871] And again: "He that offereth sacrifice of the goods of the poor is as one that sacrificeth the son in the presence of his father."[872]

[867] Ecclus. 34:27 (RSV = Sir. 34:22).
[868] Hab. 2:6.
[869] Prov. 10:2.
[870] Prov. 13:8.
[871] Isa. 61:8.
[872] Ecclus. 34:24 (RSV = Sir. 34:20).

4. The loss of spiritual goods

Finally, stealing is forbidden because the results of theft are peculiarly harmful to the thief, since they lead to his loss of other goods. It is not unlike the mixture of fire and straw: "Fire shall devour their tabernacles, who love to take bribes."[873] And it ought to be known that a thief may lose not only his own soul, but also the souls of his children, since they, too, are bound to make restitution.

[873] Job 15:34.

VIII

THOU SHALT NOT BEAR FALSE
WITNESS AGAINST THY NEIGHBOR

The Lord has forbidden anyone to injure his neighbor by deed. In this commandment he forbids us to injure him by word: *Thou shalt not bear false witness against thy neighbor.*[874]

A. Ways of bearing false witness

False witness may be given either in a court of justice or in ordinary conversation:

1. In a court of justice

In the court of justice, it may happen in three ways, according to the three persons who may violate this commandment in court.

a. A false accusation by the plaintiff: "Thou shalt not be a detractor nor a whisperer among the people."[875] Note well that it is wrong not only to speak falsely, but also to conceal the truth: "If thy brother shall offend against thee, go and rebuke him."[876]

---

[874] Cf. *Summa Theologica*, II-II, Q. 122, art. 6.
[875] Lev. 19:16.
[876] Matt. 18:15.

b. A lie told by a witness: "A false witness shall not be unpunished."[877] This commandment includes all the preceding ones, inasmuch as the false witness may himself be the murderer or the thief, and as such should be punished according to the Law.

"When after most diligent inquisition they find that the false witness hath told a lie against his brother, they shall render to him as he meant to do to his brother. . . . Thou shalt not pity him, but shalt require life for life, eye for eye, tooth for tooth, hand for hand, and foot for foot."[878] Again: "A man that beareth false witness against his neighbor is like a dart and a sword and a sharp arrow."[879]

c. An unjust sentence by the judge: "Thou shalt not . . . judge unjustly. Respect not the person of the poor, nor honor the countenance of the mighty. But judge thy neighbor according to justice."[880]

2. In ordinary conversation

In ordinary conversation, we can violate this commandment in five ways:

a. By detraction: "Detractors . . . are hateful to God."[881] Here the phrase *hateful to God* implies that nothing is as dear to a person as his good reputation: "A good name is better than great riches."[882] Detractors take away this good name:

[877] Prov. 19:5.
[878] Deut. 19:18-21.
[879] Prov. 25:18.
[880] Lev. 19:15.
[881] Rom. 1:30.
[882] Prov. 22:1.

"A serpent bites in silence, but he that backbiteth secretly is no better."[883] Thus, if detractors do not restore a man's reputation, they cannot be saved.

b. By listening to detractors willingly: "Hedge in thy ears with thorns, hear not a wicked tongue, and place doors and bars on thy mouth."[884] We should not listen deliberately to such things, but ought to turn away, showing a sad and stern countenance: "The north wind driveth away rain as doth a sad countenance a backbiting tongue."[885]

c. By gossiping: By repeating whatever they hear, gossipers break this precept: "Six things there are which the Lord hateth, and the seventh His soul detesteth: . . . him that soweth discord among brethren."[886]

d. By flattery: By speaking honeyed words, flatterers bear false witness: "The sinner is praised [by flatterers] in the desires of his soul, and the unjust man is blessed."[887] And again: "O my people, they that call thee blessed, the same shall deceive thee."[888]

e. By lying: The prohibition against bearing false witness applies to every form of falsehood: "Be not willing to make any manner of lie, for the custom thereof is no good."[889]

---

[883] Eccles. 10:11.
[884] Ecclus. 28:28 (RSV = Sir. 28:24-25).
[885] Prov. 25:23.
[886] Prov. 6:16, 19.
[887] Ps. 10:3.
[888] Isa. 3:12.
[889] Ecclus. 7:14 (RSV = Sir. 7:13).

B. Reasons lying is forbidden

1. Lying likens a person to the Devil, because a liar is as the son of the Devil. Now, we know that a man's speech reveals the region and country of his origin. Thus: "Even thy speech doth discover thee."[890] In the same way, some men are of the Devil's kind; and because they are liars, they are called *sons of the Devil,* since the Devil is "a liar and the father of lies."[891] Thus the Devil lied when he said, "No, you shall not die the death."[892]

In contrast, some other men are the children of God (who is Truth). These are the men who speak the truth.

2. Lying ruins society. Men live together in society, but this is soon rendered impossible if they do not speak the truth to one another. "Wherefore putting away lying, speak ye the truth, every man with his neighbor; for we are members one of another."[893]

3. Lying destroys the liar's reputation for the truth. He who is accustomed to telling lies is not believed, even when he speaks the truth: "What can be made clean by the unclean? And what truth can come from that which is false?"[894]

4. Lying kills the liar's soul, for "the mouth that belieth killeth the soul."[895] And again: "Thou wilt destroy all that speak a

---

[890] Matt. 26:73.
[891] John 8:44.
[892] Gen. 3:4.
[893] Eph. 4:25.
[894] Ecclus. 34:4 (RSV = Sir. 34:4).
[895] Wisd. 1:11.

lie."[896] Accordingly, it is clear that lying is a mortal sin (although it must be known that some lies may be venial).

It is a mortal sin, for instance, to lie in matters of Faith. This concerns professors, prelates, and preachers, and is the gravest of all other kinds of lies: "There shall be among you lying teachers who shall bring in sects of perdition."[897] Then there are those who lie to wrong their neighbor: "Lie not to one another."[898] These two kinds of lies, therefore, are mortal sins.

C. Reasons people lie

1. For personal advantage
There are some who lie for their own advantage, and this in a variety of ways.

a. Out of humility, people sometimes lie. This may be the case in confession, about which St. Augustine says: "Just as one must avoid concealing what he has committed, so also he must not mention what he has *not* committed." "Hath God any need of your lie?"[899] And again: "There is one that humbleth himself wickedly and his interior is full of deceit; and there is one that humbleth himself exceedingly with a great lowness."[900]

b. Because of shame, people sometimes lie, such as when someone tells a falsehood believing that he is telling the truth and then, on becoming aware of it, he is ashamed to

---

[896] Ps. 5:7 (RSV = Ps. 5:6).
[897] 2 Pet. 2:1.
[898] Col. 3:9.
[899] Job 13:7.
[900] Ecclus. 19:23-23 (RSV = Sir. 19:26).

retract the falsehood. "In no wise speak against the truth, but be ashamed of the lie of thy ignorance."[901]

c. For desired results, people sometimes lie, such as when they wish to gain or avoid something: "We have placed our hope in lies, and by falsehood we are protected."[902] And again: "He that trusteth in lies feedeth the winds."[903]

2. To benefit another, people sometimes lie, such as when they wish to free someone from death, danger, or some other loss. This must be avoided, as St. Augustine tells us: "Accept no person against thy own person, nor against thy soul a lie."[904]

3. Out of vanity, people sometimes lie. This, too, must never be done, lest the habit of such lead us to mortal sin: "For the bewitching of vanity obscureth good things."[905]

[901] Ecclus. 4:30 (RSV = Sir. 4:25).
[902] Isa. 28:15.
[903] Prov. 10:4 (No equivalent in RSV).
[904] Ecclus. 4:26 (RSV = Sir. 4:22).
[905] Wisd. 4:12.

IX

THOU SHALT NOT COVET
THY NEIGHBOR'S GOODS[906]

There is this difference between divine and human law: human law judges deeds and words, but divine law also judges thoughts. This is because human laws are made by men, who see things only exteriorly, but divine law is from God, who sees both external things and the very interior of men. "Thou art the God of my heart."[907] And again: "Man seeth those things that appear, but the Lord beholdeth the heart."[908]

A. Commandments that concern thoughts

Therefore, having considered those commandments which concern words and deeds, we now treat of those commandments which concern thoughts. For with God the intention is taken for the deed. Thus, *Thou shalt not covet* is meant to include not only the *taking* by act, but also the *intention to take*. Therefore God says: *Thou shalt not [even] covet thy neighbor's goods.*

---

[906] St. Thomas places the Tenth Commandment (in the present traditional enumeration) before the Ninth. The Tenth is wider in extension than the Ninth, which is specific.

[907] Ps. 72:26 (RSV = Ps. 73:26).

[908] 1 Kings 16:7 (RSV = 1 Sam. 16:7).

B. Reasons for this commandment
There are a number of reasons for this.

1. Man's desire has no limits, because desire itself is boundless. But he who is wise will aim at a particular end, for no one should have aimless desires: "A covetous man shall not be satisfied with money."[909] But the desires of man are never satisfied, because the heart of man is made for God. Thus says St. Augustine: "Thou hast made us for Thee, O Lord, and our heart is restless until it rests in Thee."[910] Thus, nothing less than God can satisfy the human heart: "Who satisfieth thy desire with good things."[911]

2. Covetousness destroys peace of heart, which is highly delightful. The covetous man is ever solicitous to acquire what he lacks and to hold that which he has: "The fullness of the rich will not suffer him to sleep."[912] "For where thy treasure is, there is thy heart also."[913] It was for this reason, says St. Gregory, that Christ compared riches to thorns.[914]

3. Covetousness makes riches useless to the wealthy and to others, because the covetous desire only to hold on to them: "Riches are not comely for a covetous man and a niggard."[915]

4. Covetousness destroys the equality of justice: "Thou shalt not take bribes, which blind even the wise and pervert the

---

[909] Eccles. 5:10.
[910] *Confessions,* Bk. 1, ch. 1.
[911] Ps. 102:5 (RSV = Ps. 103:5).
[912] Eccles. 5:12.
[913] Matt. 6:21.
[914] Luke 8:14.
[915] Ecclus. 14:3 (RSV = Sir. 14:3).

words of the just."[916] And again: "He that loveth gold shall not be justified."[917]

5. Covetousness destroys the love of God and neighbor. For, as St. Augustine says, "The more one loves, the less one covets." Also, the more one covets, the less one loves. "Nor despise thy dear brother for the sake of gold."[918] And just as "No man can serve two masters," so neither can he serve "God and mammon."[919]

6. Covetousness produces all kinds of wickedness. It is "the root of all evils," says St. Paul, and when this root is implanted in the heart, it brings forth murder and theft and all kinds of evil: "They that will become rich fall into temptation and into the snare of the Devil and into many unprofitable and hurtful desires which drown men in destruction and perdition. For the desire for money is the root of all evils."[920] And note, furthermore, that covetousness is a mortal sin when one covets one's neighbor's goods without reason; and even if there be a reason, it is a venial sin.

[916] Exod. 23:8.
[917] Ecclus. 31:5 (RSV = Sir. 31:5).
[918] Ecclus. 7:20 (RSV = Sir. 7:18).
[919] Matt. 6:24.
[920] 1 Tim. 6:9-10.

THOU SHALT NOT COVET THY NEIGHBOR'S WIFE

St. John says that "all that is in the world is the concupiscence of the flesh, the concupiscence of the eyes, and the pride of life."[921] Now, all that is desirable is included in these three, two of which are forbidden by the precept: "Thou shalt not covet thy neighbor's house."[922] (Here *house*, signifying "stature," refers to avarice, for "glory and wealth shall be in his house."[923] This means that he who desires his neighbor's *house*, desires honors and riches.) Thus, after the precept forbidding desire for the house of one's neighbor (i.e., honor and riches) comes the commandment prohibiting concupiscence of the flesh: *Thou shalt not covet thy neighbor's wife*.

A. Occasions when sin rules in the flesh

Because of the corruption which resulted from the Fall, none have been free from this concupiscence except Christ and the glorious Virgin. Yet, wherever there is concupiscence, there is either venial or mortal sin — if it is allowed to dominate the reason. Hence the

---

[921] 1 John 2:16.

[922] The text of Exod. 20:17 (which contains the Ninth and Tenth Commandments) reads as follows: "Thou shalt not covet thy neighbor's house; neither shalt thou desire his wife, nor his servant, nor his handmaid, nor his ox, nor his ass, nor anything that is his."

[923] Ps. 111:3 (RSV = Ps. 112:3).

precept does not say, "Let sin not be." For it is written: "I know that there dwelleth not in me (i.e., in my flesh) that which is good."[924]

1. When concupiscence reigns in the heart (by our consenting to it), sin rules in the flesh. Therefore St. Paul adds "so as to obey the lusts thereof" to the words: "Let not sin reign in your mortal body."[925] Accordingly the Lord says: "whosoever shall look on a woman to lust after her hath already committed adultery with her in his heart."[926] For with God, the intention is taken for the act.

2. When our heart's concupiscence is expressed in words, sin rules in the flesh: "Out of the abundance of the heart the mouth speaketh."[927] And again: "Let no evil speech proceed from your mouth."[928] Therefore, one is not without sin who composes titillating songs. Even the philosophers thought this, and poets who wrote amatory verses were sent into exile.

3. When our members are made to serve iniquity (at the behest of desires), sin rules in the flesh: "You have yielded your members to serve uncleanness and iniquity unto iniquity."[929] These, therefore, are the progressive steps of concupiscence.

B. How concupiscence can be overcome
We must realize that the avoidance of concupiscence demands much labor, for concupiscence is grounded in something within us.

[924] Rom. 7:18.
[925] Rom. 6:12.
[926] Matt. 5:28.
[927] Matt. 12:34.
[928] Eph. 4:29.
[929] Rom. 6:19.

It is as hard as trying to capture an enemy in one's own household. However, there are four ways to overcome concupiscence.

1. By fleeing its external occasions (such as, for instance, bad company and whatever else may be an occasion for this sin), concupiscence can be overcome: "Gaze not upon a maiden lest her beauty be a stumbling block to thee. . . . Look not around about thee in the ways of the city, nor wander up and down in the streets thereof. Turn away thy face from a woman dressed up and gaze not about upon another's beauty. For many have perished by the beauty of a woman, and hereby lust is enkindled as a fire."[930] And again: "Can a man hide fire in his bosom and his garments not burn?"[931] Therefore, Lot was commanded to flee: "Neither stay thou in all the country about."[932]

2. By mortification of the flesh and by not giving an opening to thoughts which of themselves are the occasion of lustful desires, concupiscence can be overcome: "I chastise my body and bring it into subjection."[933]

3. By perseverance in prayer, concupiscence can be overcome: "Unless the Lord build the house, they labor in vain who build it."[934] Also: "I knew that I could not otherwise be continent, except God gave it."[935] Again: "This kind is not cast out save by prayer and fasting."[936]

---

[930] Ecclus. 9:5-9 (RSV = Sir. 9:5-8).
[931] Prov. 6:27.
[932] Gen. 19:17.
[933] 1 Cor. 9:27.
[934] Ps. 126:1 (RSV = Ps. 127:1).
[935] Wisd. 8:21.
[936] Mark 9:29.

All this is not unlike a fight between two persons, one of whom you desire to win, the other to lose. You must sustain the one and withdraw all support from the other. So, also, between the spirit and the flesh there is a continual combat. Now, if you wish the spirit to win, you must assist it by prayer and resist the flesh by such means as fasting (for by fasting the flesh is weakened).

4. By keeping oneself busy with wholesome occupations, concupiscence is overcome: "Idleness hath taught much evil."[937] Again: "This was the iniquity of Sodom thy sister: pride, fullness of bread, abundance, and idleness."[938] St. Jerome says: "Be always busy in doing something good, so that the Devil may find you ever occupied." Moreover, as he tells us, study of the Scriptures is the best of all occupations: "Love to study the Scriptures, and you will not love the vices of the flesh."

---

[937] Ecclus. 33:29 (RSV = Sir. 33:27).
[938] Ezek. 16:49.

XI

SUMMARY OF THE COMMANDMENTS

So these are the ten precepts to which our Lord referred when He said, "If thou wilt enter into life, keep the Commandments."[939] There are two main principles of these Commandments: love of God and love of neighbor.

A. Love of God
If we are to love God, we must necessarily do three things:

1. We must have no other God
In support of this is the commandment *Thou shalt not have strange gods before me.*

2. We must give God all honor
Thus it is commanded: *Thou shalt not take the name of the Lord thy God in vain.*

3. We must freely take our rest in God
Hence: *Remember that thou keep holy the Sabbath day.*

B. Love of neighbor
To love God worthily, we must first of all love our neighbor.

[939] Matt. 19:17.

249

1. We must honor our parents

So we have the commandment *Honor thy father and thy mother.*

2. We must refrain from harming our neighbor

a. By act

Thus we have those commandments which forbid harm to our neighbor in act: *Thou shalt not kill* concerns our neighbor's person; *Thou shalt not commit adultery* concerns the person united in marriage to our neighbor; and *Thou shalt not steal* concerns our neighbor's external goods.

b. By word and by thought

We are also commanded to avoid injury to our neighbor both by word (*Thou shalt not bear false witness*) and by thought (*Thou shalt not covet thy neighbor's goods* and *Thou shalt not covet thy neighbor's wife*).

Part 4

How the Church Nourishes Christians

The Sacraments

I

THE SACRAMENTS IN GENERAL

We shall first consider the Sacraments of the Church under one heading, since they all pertain to the effects of grace.

A. The nature of a sacrament

1. A sacrament is a sign of a sacred thing

First, we must know that which St. Augustine wrote in the tenth book of *The City of God:* "a sacrament is a sacred thing" or "the sign of a sacred thing."[940] Even in the Old Law there were certain sacraments (i.e., signs of sacred things) such as the paschal lamb and other legal, sacred signs (or sacraments) which, however, did not cause grace but only signified or indicated the grace of Christ.

The Apostle calls these sacraments "weak and needy elements."[941] They were *needy* because they did not contain grace and *weak* because they could not confer grace.

✠ As St. Augustine says, in them the merits of Christ brought about salvation in a more hidden manner under the cover of visible things.

---

[940] *The City of God*, Bk. 10, ch. 5.
[941] Gal. 4:9.

2. A sacrament is a visible form of an invisible grace

The Sacraments of the New Law, on the other hand, both contain grace and confer it. A sacrament of the New Law is a visible form of invisible grace. Thus, the exterior washing which takes place when water is poured in Baptism represents that interior cleansing which takes away sin by virtue of the sacrament of Baptism.

B. The number of the Sacraments

There are seven Sacraments of the New Law: namely, Baptism, Confirmation, the Eucharist, Penance, the Anointing of the Sick, Holy Orders, and Matrimony. The first five of these Sacraments are intended to bring about the perfection of the individual man in himself; the other two sacraments — Holy Orders and Matrimony — are so constituted that they perfect and multiply the entire Church.

C. The effects of the Sacraments

The spiritual life conforms to the physical life. In the physical life man is perfected in three chief ways: (1) *by generation*, in that he is born into this world; (2) *by growth*, through which he is brought up into stature and perfect strength; and (3) *by food*, which sustains his life and powers. This would suffice were it not that man falls ill and then needs his health to be restored (4) *by healing*. These same needs are found in the spiritual life:

1. Regeneration

First, man needs that regeneration or rebirth which is brought through the sacrament of Baptism: "Unless a man be born again of water and the Holy Spirit, he cannot enter into the kingdom of God."[942]

---

[942] John 3:5.

2. Spiritual growth

Second, it is necessary that man develop perfect strength which is, as it were, a spiritual growth. This, indeed, comes to him in the sacrament of Confirmation. It is like the strengthening the Apostles received when the Holy Spirit came upon them and confirmed them. The Lord had said to them: "But stay in the city of Jerusalem till you be endued with power from on high."[943]

3. Nourishment

The third similarity is that man must be fed with spiritual food in the sacrament of the Eucharist: "Unless you eat the flesh of the Son of Man and drink His blood, you shall not have life in you."[944]

4. Spiritual healing

Fourth, man must be healed spiritually in the sacrament of Penance: "Heal, O Lord, my soul, for I have sinned against Thee."[945]

5. Bodily and spiritual healing

Fifth, man is healed both in soul and in body in the sacrament of the Anointing of the Sick: "Is any man sick among you? Let him bring in the priests of the church and let them pray over him, anointing him with oil in the name of the Lord. The prayer of faith shall save the sick man, and the Lord shall raise him up; and if he be in sins, they shall be forgiven him."[946]

6. The good of the Church

Finally, two sacraments — Holy Orders and Matrimony — were instituted for the common good of the Church. Through Holy

[943] Luke 24:49.
[944] John 6:54 (RSV = John 6:53).
[945] Ps. 40:5 (RSV = Ps. 41:4).
[946] James 5:14-15.

Orders, the Church is ruled and spiritually multiplied. Through Matrimony, it is increased physically in numbers.

D. Characteristics of all the Sacraments

The Seven Sacraments have some things which they all hold in common and some things which are proper to each one.

1. The conferring of grace is common to each sacrament.

2. Words and physical acts are essential to each sacrament. Christ, the author of the Sacraments, is the Word made flesh. Just as the flesh of Christ was sanctified and has the power of sanctifying because of the Word united to itself, so also the Sacraments are made holy and have the power of sanctifying through the words which accompany the action. Thus, St. Augustine says: "The word is joined to the element and the sacrament is made."[947]

> **a. The form of a sacrament** consists of the words by which that sacrament is sanctified.

> **b. The matter of a sacrament** consists of those things which are sanctified. Water, for example, is the matter of Baptism, and holy chrism is the matter of Confirmation.

3. A minister is required for each sacrament. The minister confers the sacrament with the intention of doing that which the Church intends.

The sacrament is not brought into being if any one of these three requirements is lacking (i.e., if there is lacking the due

---

[947] *In Joan.*, Tract. 80.3.

form of the words, if the matter is not present, or if the minister does not intend to confer the sacrament).

4. The interior disposition of the recipient plays a role in each sacrament. Thus, the effect of the sacrament can be impeded through the fault of the recipient, such as when a person feigns to receive it but has a heart unprepared to receive it worthily. Although he actually receives the sacrament, such a person does not receive the effect of the sacrament: the grace of the Holy Spirit. "For the Holy Spirit of discipline will flee from the deceitful."[948]

On the other hand, however, there are some who never receive sacramentally, yet who receive the effect of a sacrament because of a devotion toward the sacrament which they may have in desire or in a vow.

E. Unique characteristics of particular sacraments

There are some things which are characteristic of each individual sacrament.

1. Sacraments which impress a character on the soul

Certain sacraments impress on the soul a character which is a certain spiritual sign distinct from the other sacraments. Such are the sacraments of Holy Orders, Baptism, and Confirmation. A sacrament which impresses character on the soul is never repeated in a person who has once received it. Thus, he who is baptized need never again receive this sacrament. Neither can he who has been confirmed receive Confirmation again, nor he who has been ordained repeat his Ordination. The reason is that the character which each of these sacraments impresses is indelible.

[948] Wisd. 1:5.

2. Sacraments which do not impress a character on the soul

In the other sacraments, however, a character is not impressed on the recipient. Hence they can be repeated as far as the person is concerned, but not as far as the matter is concerned. Thus, one can frequently receive Penance, frequently receive the Eucharist, and can be anointed more than once with the Anointing of the Sick. Likewise, a person can be married more than once.

Yet, regarding the matter, the same Host cannot be frequently consecrated, nor ought the oil of the sick be frequently blessed.

II

THE SACRAMENTS IN PARTICULAR

Having considered the Sacraments in general, it is now necessary to say something about each one in particular.

A. Baptism

First we consider Baptism, about which the following must be known:

1. The matter of Baptism is natural water, and it makes no difference whether it is cold or warm. One cannot, however, baptize in artificial waters (such as rose water).

2. The form of Baptism is: "I baptize thee in the name of the Father and of the Son and of the Holy Spirit."

3. The minister of Baptism ordinarily is the priest, whose office it is to baptize. In case of necessity, however, not only a deacon but also any layperson (even a pagan or a heretic) can baptize as long as he observes the form specified by the Church and intends to act according to the intention of the Church. If someone is baptized by such persons but *not* in a case of necessity, he has received the sacrament and must not again be baptized, but the grace of the sacrament was not received because such persons are not truly deputed to baptize other than in cases of necessity. Hence, they act contrary to the law of the Church regulating the Sacraments.

4. The effect of Baptism is to remit both actual sin and Original Sin as well as all guilt and punishment which they incur. No kind of punishment must be enjoined for past sins upon those just newly baptized. Hence, those who die immediately after Baptism are admitted to the glory of God without delay. Therefore the effect of Baptism is the opening of the gates of Paradise.

5. Errors concerning Baptism have arisen:

a. The Solentiani received a baptism not of water but of the spirit. Against them the Lord says: "Unless a man be born again of water and the Holy Spirit, he cannot enter into the kingdom of God."[949]

b. The Donatists rebaptized those baptized by Catholics. Against them is written: "One Faith, one Baptism."[950]

c. Those who claim that a man in the state of sin cannot baptize also err. Against them it is said: "He upon whom thou shalt see the Spirit descending and remaining upon Him, He it is that baptizeth."[951] It is thus seen that a minister who is himself evil does not invalidate either this or any of the other sacraments because it is Christ who, by the merits of His Passion, gives to each sacrament its efficacy; and He is good.

[949] John 3:5.
[950] Eph. 4:5.
[951] John 1:33.

d. The Pelagians err when they say that children are not freed from Original Sin by Baptism, but rather through their baptismal regeneration are merely admitted as adopted children of God into the kingdom, being translated from a good state to a better one.

B. Confirmation

1. The matter of Confirmation is chrism made from oil (signifying the bright luster of conscience) and from balsam (signifying the odor of a good name). Both oils are blessed by the bishop.

2. The form of Confirmation is: "I sign thee with the Sign of the Cross, and I confirm thee with the chrism of salvation, in the name of the Father and of the Son and of the Holy Spirit. Amen."

3. The minister of Confirmation is solely the bishop. It is not licit for a priest to anoint on the forehead with chrism those who are to be confirmed.[952]

4. The effect of Confirmation is that the Holy Spirit is imparted to give strength, just as the Holy Spirit was given to the Apostles on the day of Pentecost. Thus, the Christian must boldly confess the name of Christ.

The person who is confirmed is anointed on the forehead (wherein is the seat of fear) so that he will not blush to confess either the name of Christ or especially the Cross of Christ,

[952] In the Latin Church, the ordinary minister of Confirmation is the bishop. However, in virtue of Canon 882, a priest can also validly confer this sacrament in certain circumstances.

which to the Jews was a scandal and to the pagans foolishness.[953] For this reason, the person who is confirmed is signed with the Sign of the Cross.

5. Errors concerning Confirmation

Certain Greeks have erred about this sacrament by saying that it could be administered by one who is only a priest. Against this it is said that the Apostles sent the Apostles Peter and John to impose hands upon those who had been baptized by Philip the deacon, and they received the Holy Spirit. Now, the bishops of the Church are in the places of the Apostles; and in their place also do they impose hands when the sacrament of Confirmation is administered.

C. The Holy Eucharist

1. The matter of the Eucharist is wheaten bread and wine made from the grape mixed with a little water so that the water becomes part of the wine. The water signifies the faithful who are incorporated into Christ. The *matter* for this sacrament cannot be anything other than wheaten bread and wine from the grape.

2. The form of the Eucharist is the very words of Christ: "This is my body" and "This is the cup of my blood, the blood of the new and everlasting covenant. It will be shed for you and for all, so that sins may be forgiven." These words spoken by the priest in the person of Christ bring into being this sacrament.

3. The minister of the Eucharist is the priest, and no one else can consecrate this matter into the Body of Christ.

[953] 1 Cor. 1:23.

262

4. The effects of the Eucharist

a. Christ becomes physically present
In virtue of the above words, bread is changed into the Body of Christ and wine into His Blood, so that Christ is entirely contained under the appearances of bread, which remain without a subject, and He is entirely contained under the appearances of wine. Moreover, under each part of the consecrated host and of the consecrated wine, Christ is totally present even after the separation is made.

b. The communicant is united with Christ
In the soul of one who worthily receives this sacrament, its second effect is to bring about the union of that man with Christ, as He himself says: "He that eateth my flesh and drinketh my blood abideth in me, and I in him."[954] And since man is incorporated with Christ and united to His members through grace, it follows that through this sacrament, grace is increased in those who receive it worthily. Therefore, in this sacrament there are three aspects: 1) the *sacramentum tantum* (that which is the sacrament alone: the species of bread and wine); 2) the *res et sacramentum* (the true Body of Christ); and 3) the *res tantum* (the unity of the Mystical Body, the Church), which this sacrament both signifies and causes.

5. Errors concerning the Eucharist
There have been many errors regarding this sacrament.

a. Berengarius said that the true Body of Christ is not present in the Eucharist, but rather, the Eucharist is only a sign

[954] John 6:57 (RSV = John 6:56).

of it. Against this is written: "For my flesh is meat indeed; and my blood is drink indeed."[955]

b. The Arrodinici offer in their sacrament bread and cheese because they say that men at first made offerings of the fruits of the earth and of their flocks. Against this, however, stands the fact that the Lord, the institutor of this sacrament, gave His disciples bread and wine.

c. The Cataphrygians and the Praeputiati drew the blood of an infant from tiny punctures in his body. Mixing this with flour, they made a bread out of it. They claimed that thus they consecrated the sacrament. This is more like the sacrifices of demons than that of Christ: "And they shed innocent blood . . . which they sacrificed to the idols of Canaan."[956]

d. The Aquarians offer only water in their sacrifices. But against this are the words from the mouth of Wisdom, which is Christ: "Drink the wine which I have mingled for you."[957]

e. The Poor People of Lyons held that any just man can consecrate the Eucharist. Against this error is the fact that the Lord gave to the Apostles the power to celebrate this sacrament. Therefore, only those who receive this power in a certain succession from the Apostles can consecrate this sacrament.

---

[955] John 6:56 (RSV = John 6:55).
[956] Ps. 105:38 (RSV = Ps. 106:38).
[957] Prov. 9:5.

D. Penance[958]

1. The matter of Penance consists, as it were, of the acts of the penitent, which are called the three parts of Penance.

a. Heartfelt contrition is the first part, by which the sinner is sorry for the sins he has committed and determines not to sin again.

b. Confession is the second part. In it the sinner confesses to the priest all the sins of which he is mindful and all of them at one time to one priest, not dividing them among a number of priests.

c. Satisfaction is the third part, which is enjoined according to the judgment of the priest and which consists especially in fasting, prayer, and almsgiving.

2. The form of Penance consists of the words of absolution which the priest speaks when he says: "I absolve thee."

3. The minister of Penance is the priest having authority to absolve, which authority is either ordinary or by commission of his superior.

4. The effect of Penance is absolution from sin.

5. Errors concerning Penance
The Novatians say that anyone who has sinned after having been baptized cannot receive pardon through the sacrament of Penance. Against this are the words: "Be mindful therefore

---

[958] Or *Confession*, now called *Reconciliation*.

from whence thou art fallen; do penance and do the first works."[959]

E. The Anointing of the Sick

1. The matter of the Anointing of the Sick is olive oil blessed by the bishop. This sacrament should be received only by those who are in danger of death through sickness. They are to be anointed in the places of the five senses: on the eyes, because they are the organs of sight; on the ears, because of hearing; on the nostrils, because of smell; on the lips, because of taste or speech; on the hands because of touch; and on the feet because of walking.

2. The form of the Anointing of the Sick is: "Through this anointing and through His most divine mercy, may the Lord forgive thee whatever thou hast committed through sight . . ." (and so on for the other senses).

3. The minister of the Anointing of the Sick is the priest.

4. The effect of the Anointing of the Sick is healing for both mind and body.

5. Errors concerning the Anointing of the Sick
It is said that the Elaeonitae anointed their dying with oil, balsam, and water and that they accompanied the anointing with invocations in Hebrew pronounced over the head of the sick. However, this is contrary to the form handed down by St. James, as given above.

[959] Apoc. 2:5 (RSV = Rev. 2:5).

F. Holy Orders

There are seven orders — namely, priesthood, diaconate, subdiaconate, acolyte, exorcist, lector, and porter. Tonsure (clerkship, *clericatus*) is not an order, but a formal profession of giving one's life to the divine ministry. The episcopate is rather a dignity than an order.

1. The matter of Holy Orders is that matter which is handed over to the candidate at the conferring of the order. Thus, for example, priesthood is conferred by the handing over of the chalice. Likewise, each order is conferred by the handing over of that matter which in a special way pertains to the ministry of that particular order.

2. The form of Holy Orders is this: "Receive the power to offer sacrifice in the Church for the living and the dead." Similarly, power is conferred in the other orders.

3. The minister of Holy Orders is the bishop who confers the orders.

4. The effect of Holy Orders is an increase of grace for the performance of the duties of a worthy minister of Christ.

5. Errors concerning Holy Orders
Arius erroneously taught that the priesthood could not be distinguished from the episcopate.

G. Matrimony

Matrimony is a sign of the union between Christ and the Church.

1. The efficient cause of Matrimony is the mutual consent expressed in words effective in the present by the parties.

2. The threefold good of Matrimony includes:

a. The birth of children and their education to the worship of God.

b. Fidelity, which one spouse must render to the other.

c. Its sacramental character. The indivisibility of Matrimony shows forth the indivisible union of Christ and His Church.

3. Errors concerning Matrimony

a. Tatian condemned marriage. Against such it is written: "If thou take a wife, thou hast not sinned."[960]

b. Jovinian erroneously made marriage equal to virginity.

c. The Nicolaitians mutually exchanged their wives. There were also many other heretics who taught and worked impurities. Against them are the words of St. Paul: "Marriage honorable in all, and the bed undefiled."[961]

---

[960] 1 Cor. 7:28.
[961] Heb. 13:4.

III

THE GIFTS OF THE SACRAMENTS

By the reception of these Seven Sacraments, man is led to future eternal glory, which consists in seven gifts: three of the soul and four of the body.

A. The three gifts of the soul

1. The vision of God in His essence is the first gift that is given to the soul, according to the words: "We shall see Him as He is."[962]

2. Comprehension, or the understanding of God as the reward of our merits, is the second gift of the soul: "So run that you may obtain."[963]

3. Perfect enjoyment is the third gift of the soul, and in this we shall have full happiness in God: "Then shalt thou abound in delights of the Almighty, and shalt lift up thy face to God."[964]

---

[962] 1 John 3:2.
[963] 1 Cor. 9:24.
[964] Job 22:26.

B. The four gifts of the body

1. Impassibilty[965] is the first gift which shall be enjoyed by the body, for "this corruptible must put on incorruption."[966]

2. Brilliancy is the second gift of the body: "Then shall the just shine as the sun in the kingdom of their Father."[967]

3. Agility is the third gift of the body, through which those saved can instantly be present wherever they wish: "They shall run to and fro like sparks among the reeds."[968]

4. Subtlety is the fourth gift of the body, whereby those saved can penetrate wherever they desire: "It is sown a natural body; it shall rise a spiritual body."[969]

To all of which may He lead us,
who liveth and reigneth
forever and ever! Amen.

---

[965] The state of being beyond the reach of suffering or harm.
[966] 1 Cor. 15:53.
[967] Matt. 13:43.
[968] Wisd. 3:7.
[969] 1 Cor. 15:44.

APPENDIX

The following pages constitute a complete outline of each of the sections of this book and include subheadings not found in the table of contents. Use this outline as a guide in reading and studying the text.

What Christians Believe

THE APOSTLES' CREED

a. The wicked
  1. Some will be condemned but not judged
  2. Some will be both condemned and judged
b. The good
  1. Some will be saved and will not be judged
  2. Some will be both saved and judged
3. They will be judged on all their works
C. Why the judgment is to be feared
  1. Because of the Judge's wisdom
  2. Because of the Judge's power
  3. Because of the Judge's inflexible justice
  4. Because of the Judge's anger
D. How we are to prepare for the judgment
  1. Good deeds
  2. Confession and repentance
  3. Almsgiving
  4. Charity

A. Characteristics of the Holy Spirit
  1. The Lord
  2. The Giver of Life
  3. Who proceeds from the Father and the Son
  4. With the Father and the Son He is worshiped and glorified
  5. He has spoken through the prophets
B. Fruits of the Holy Spirit
  1. Forgiveness of sins
  2. Enlightenment
  3. Adherence to the Commandments
  4. Hope
  5. Counsel

A. The Church is one
  1. From the unity of faith
  2. From the unity of hope
  3. From the unity of charity
B. The Church is holy
  1. The Church as an assembly of the good
  2. The Church sanctifies its members
    a. By washing them
    b. By anointing them

D. Qualities of the bodies of the damned
    1. Passiblity
    2. Darkness
    3. Heaviness
    4. Carnality

A. The nature of the eternal life of the blessed
    1. Perfect vision of God
    2. Perfect knowledge of God
    3. Perfect praise of God
    4. Perfect fulfillment of desires
        a. Pleasure
        b. Honors
        c. Knowledge
    5. Perfect security
    6. Companionship of the blessed
B. The nature of the eternal death of the wicked
    1. Separation from God
    2. Remorse of conscience
    3. Intensity of the pains of sense
    4. Despair of salvation

How Christians Should Pray

THE LORD'S PRAYER

    A. Conditions required for prayer
        1. Confidence
        2. Rectitude
        3. Order
        4. Devoutness
        5. Humility
    B. Benefits of prayer
        1. It remedies evils
        2. It obtains that which we desire
        3. It establishes friendship with God

    A. Why we call God *Father*
        1. He created us
        2. He governs us
        3. He adopted us
    B. What we owe God as our Father
        1. Honor
            a. In reference to Him
            b. In reference to ourselves
            c. In reference to our neighbor
        2. Imitation
            a. By loving Him
            b. By showing mercy
            c. By being perfect
        3. Obedience
            a. Because of His dominion
            b. Because of His example
            c. Because obedience is good for us
        4. Patience

THE HAIL MARY

    A. The superiority of angels over men
        1. In dignity
        2. In close association with God
        3. In the fullness of divine grace
    B. The superiority of the Blessed Virgin over the angels
        1. In dignity
            a. Grace filled her soul
            b. Grace overflowed into her body
            c. Grace overflows from her onto all mankind
        2. In her close association with God
            a. In her relation to God the Father
            b. In her relation to God the Son
            c. In her relation to God the Holy Spirit
        3. In the fullness of divine grace
            a. Mary was immune from the curse on woman
            b. She was immune from the curse on man
            c. She was immune from the curse on man *and* woman
    C. Only the Virgin's Fruit affords what Eve sought in her fruit
        1. Likeness to God
        2. Delight
        3. Beauty

How Christians Should Live

THE COMMANDMENTS

1. To confirm something that is said
2. To sanctify
3. To expel our adversary
4. To confess God's name
    a. By word of mouth
    b. By our works
5. To defend ourselves
6. To make our works complete

    A. Reasons for this commandment
        1. To put aside errors
            a. The error of those who deny the first creation
            b. The error of those who deny the second creation
        2. To instruct us in our faith in the Redeemer
        3. To strengthen the promise of rest
        4. To increase our love
        5. To exercise works of kindliness
    B. How to keep the Sabbath holy
        1. The meanings of *holy*
            a. *Holy* signifies "pure"
            b. *Holy* signifies "consecrated"
        2. Things to avoid on the Sabbath
            a. Servile work
                1. Impermissible servile work
                2. Reasons that permit servile work
                    on the Sabbath
                    a. Necessity
                    b. Service of the Church
                    c. The good of our neighbor
                    d. The authority of our superiors
            b. Sin
            c. Idleness
        3. Things to do on the Sabbath and feast days
            a. Offer sacrifice
                1. Our soul as sacrifice
                2. Our body as sacrifice
                3. Our possessions as sacrifice
            b. Hear God's word
            c. Contemplate divine things
                1. Rest in divine contemplation

2. Rests that precede divine contemplation
   a. Rest from the turmoil of sin
   b. Rest from the passions of the flesh
   c. Rest from the occupations of the world
3. Eternal rest

   A. Reasons we should honor our parents
      1. Their union with us
      2. The benefits they have given us
         a. Being
         b. Nourishment and support
         c. Instruction
   B. Obligations to parents that arise from these benefits
      1. Honor, because they gave us existence
      2. Support, because they gave us nourishment
      3. Obedience, because they gave us instruction
   C. Rewards for honoring our parents
      1. Grace and glory
      2. A long life
      3. Grateful and pleasing children
      4. A praiseworthy reputation
      5. Riches
   D. Others who deserve the reverence due to fathers
      1. The Apostles and saints
      2. Our superiors in the Church
      3. Rulers and kings
      4. Our benefactors
      5. Old men

   A. Killing
      1. Errors regarding killing
         a. The killing of animals
         b. The execution of criminals
         c. Suicide
      2. Ways of killing a man's body
         a. By one's own hand
         b. By word of mouth
         c. By helping another kill
         d. By consenting to another's death
         e. By not preventing another's death

1. They destroy the soul
2. They destroy life
3. They waste substance
4. They defile offspring
5. They destroy honor

  A. Ways of stealing
    1. By taking stealthily
    2. By taking with violence
    3. By not paying wages that are due
    4. By fraudulent buying and selling
    5. By buying promotions
  B. Reasons stealing is forbidden
    1. The gravity of the sin
    2. The unique dangers of theft
    3. The uselessness of stolen goods
    4. The loss of spiritual goods

  A. Ways of bearing false witness
    1. In a court of justice
      a. A false accusation by the plaintiff
      b. A lie told by a witness
      c. An unjust sentence by the judge
    2. In ordinary conversation
      a. By detraction
      b. By listening to detractors willingly
      c. By gossiping
      d. By flattery
      e. By lying
  B. Reasons lying is forbidden
    1. Lying likens a person to the Devil
    2. Lying ruins society
    3. Lying destroys the liar's reputation for the truth
    4. Lying kills the liar's soul
  C. Reasons people lie
    1. For personal advantage
      a. Out of humility
      b. Because of shame
      c. For desired results
    2. To benefit another
    3. Out of vanity

How the Church Nourishes Christians

THE SACRAMENTS

Biographical Note

ST. THOMAS AQUINAS
(1225-1274)

Scholar and saint! Certainly it is a rare combination today, but St. Thomas Aquinas was both. He devoted his entire life to comprehending God's Revelation — through reason, contemplation, and prayer — and to living in conformity with the call of that Revelation.

Born of an illustrious and politically prominent family in Naples, St. Thomas was educated at the famous Monte Cassino Abbey and at the University of Naples. In 1244, against the wishes of his family, he entered the Dominican Order.

The Dominicans sent Thomas to the University of Paris to study with the renowned Aristotelian scholar Albert the Great. In 1252, Thomas began his teaching career which involved him in every major intellectual debate of the time. Through many formal academic disputations, through his preaching, and in over 100 written volumes, St. Thomas gave his reason unreservedly to the service of Christian Revelation. Relying heavily on the Greek philosopher Aristotle, Thomas showed that Christian Faith is credible, defensible, and intelligible.

Moreover, St. Thomas's prodigious scholarship nurtured his own spiritual development. He prayed intensely and was known to suffer the terrible spiritual trials and sublime consolations of the true ascetic and contemplative.

St. Thomas died at the early age of 50, on March 7, 1274. He was canonized in 1323 and proclaimed a Doctor of the Universal Church in 1567.

In his encyclical *Æterni Patris* (dated August 4, 1879), Pope Leo XIII called on all men to "restore the golden wisdom of St. Thomas and to spread it far and wide for the defense and beauty of the Catholic Faith, for the good of society, and for the advantage of all sciences."

An Invitation

Reader, the book that you hold in your hands was published by Sophia Institute Press. Sophia Institute seeks to nurture the spiritual, moral, and cultural life of souls and to spread the Gospel of Christ in conformity with the authentic teachings of the Roman Catholic Church.

Our press fulfills this mission by offering translations, reprints, and new publications that afford readers a rich source of the enduring wisdom of mankind.

We also operate two popular online Catholic resources: CrisisMagazine.com and CatholicExchange.com.

Crisis Magazine provides insightful cultural analysis that arms readers with the arguments necessary for navigating the ideological and theological minefields of the day. *Catholic Exchange* provides world news from a Catholic perspective as well as daily devotionals and articles that will help you to grow in holiness and live a life consistent with the teachings of the Church.

Sophia Institute Press also serves as the publisher for the Thomas More College of Liberal Arts and Holy Spirit College. Both colleges provide university-level education under the guiding light of Catholic teaching. If you know a young person seeking a college that takes seriously the adventure of learning and the quest for truth, please bring these institutions to his attention.

www.SophiaInstitute.com
www.CatholicExchange.com
www.CrisisMagazine.com